Wrapped In Stillness

A Personal Retreat Guide

Wrapped In Stillness

A Personal Retreat Guide

Windy City Publishers
2118 Plum Grove Rd., #349
Rolling Meadows, IL 60008
www.windycitypublishers.com

Published in the United States of America

10 9 8 7 6 5 4 3 2 1

First Edition: 2013

Library of Congress Control Number:
2013946104

ISBN:
978-1-935766-87-2

Windy City Publishers
Chicago

Wrapped
In Stillness

A Personal Retreat Guide

Laurie Guest

WINDY CITY
PUBLISHERS

To Tom, Evan, & Ellie

My reason for being.

Comments from Readers

"After your presentation, I made the commitment to engage in my first ever personal retreat. I sat on my sunporch with a journal and notes from your session and began asking myself questions. I spent eight hours thinking, reading and praying. I am very happy with this process and it changed my life. Thank you!"

~Dana, Freeport, IL

"When I read your chapter on finding closure I was reminded of my grandfather. We planned to build a horse farm together. But he died suddenly when I was still a young girl and I gave up the goal. After reading your book I decided to open the door back up on the dream more than fifty years later. My husband and I now own a horse-breeding farm and I tell people all the time it was because of your book. My grandpa started the dream and now I'm going to finish it."

~Sharon, Little Rock, AR

"I wasn't sure what a personal retreat would be like but Laurie's book was exactly what I needed to get my thoughts in order. When I finished reading the book I realized that I needed this quiet alone time to reflect on the past and to plan what I wanted for myself in the future."

~Kristi, DeKalb, IL

"Laurie's book gave me the permission to take care of myself. She gave me the inspiration to use some of her exercises to heal myself and get my life back on track. I am so incredibly grateful to her for learning how to honor myself. I cannot contribute to my family, my job or my community when I am depleted. When I am full of energy I can give to those around me. It is not selfish to take a personal retreat day or even several days. It is actually the only responsible thing to do when you are stuck, off course, overwhelmed or exhausted. This book helps you say YES to the possibilities of your future! Thank you, Laurie, for helping me relaunch a new, happy life. Your guidance and exercises were life changing and inspirational!"

~Lori, Frankfort, IL

Contents

Planning Your Life & Finding Focus

Rejuvenation & Celebration

WRAP UP & RESOURCES

Introduction

"A retreat is about
stepping out
of your ordinary
existence to listen
and attune to your
truest and most
authentic self."

~Jennifer Louden
Author & Retreat Expert

What Is a Retreat?

A personal retreat is time set aside to reflect and explore your intentions and replenish your energy. It is a break from the stresses and time constraints of daily life and a chance to focus your attention solely on you. While there are no hard and fast rules about how to conduct a personal retreat, it does require a plan, which should include a comfortable environment and relevant resources.

Uncluttering your mind and providing time and space for productive thought is the goal of the personal retreat.

THERE ARE MANY KINDS OF PERSONAL RETREATS

You have almost infinite options in designing your personal retreat, which can be adapted to your objective and available resources. You may choose a personal retreat as short as two minutes or as long as several days. My personal favorite is the single-day retreat. It provides just enough time to gain meaningful traction with my objective.

In addition to determining the length of your retreat, you'll want to decide on an appropriate location. Some people prefer staying home and retreating to a quiet room, patio, or self-created retreat space. Others may prefer a community park, a library, or the home of a friend who is away on vacation. Nature getaways are a favorite destination for those who prefer arboretums, mountains, or national parks. My favorite location, by far, is a retreat center, a bed and breakfast, or a cabin on the beach.

While it is absolutely possible to plan a personal retreat that includes others, this book was written to guide those seeking time alone with their own thoughts. For many of us, time spent in the company of ourselves is a novelty. Alone time can be the basis for a breakthrough in our thinking.

The more you retreat, the more creative you'll become in the design of your retreat. Over time, some people find they become braver in the choice of a location or in the exercises they perform.

Choosing a duration and environment that are right for you are critical components of a successful personal retreat. It is all about you. Pick a place you really enjoy. Stay long enough to make progress toward your objective. I know I have made the right choices when I settle in with a sigh of contentment.

Every personal retreat should begin with the question, "What is the reason for my retreat?" Your answer provides the foundational intention of your retreat and ensures a more productive outcome. An intention is a commitment to a purpose. By stating your purpose to yourself, you provide an objective for your retreat. You might achieve that objective by simply allowing your mind to relax and wander. You might choose to process emotions or explore the pros and cons of a decision. Your intention for each personal retreat is up to you; but intention, even if it changes during the course of your retreat, should be in place when you begin.

HOW CAN THIS BOOK HELP?

Think of this book as a global positioning satellite (GPS) for a perfect personal retreat. Just like a GPS in a car, you program your destination and allow yourself to be wrapped in stillness. Let your gut instinct and your intention guide you—one turn at a time. This book is designed to help you sort out your thoughts and navigate a path toward the future you desire. Think of this guide as close friend, a confidant who asks just the right questions without judging your honest answers.

You will easily relate to the short anecdotes and thought-provoking questions within these pages. They are intended to kindle your thought process and help you analyze your life. They will help you design a personal retreat that fits your needs perfectly.

I wrote this book because I am passionate about the value of personal retreats. It is my strong belief that if everyone invested time in their future through personal reflection, their lives would be impacted dramatically.

Focusing on self is not selfish.
Taking care of you is the foundation
of being able to care for others.

HOW DO I USE THIS BOOK?

You may use this book any way you want; there is no right or wrong way to use it. It is divided into sections for convenience. Please note that the self-reflective chapters do not have to be read in order. Sometimes reading several chapters and then going back to focus on the areas you marked may be a productive way to use the book.

When you finish a chapter, read through the questions and ignore the ones that don't apply; skip over those you don't like, then dig into the rest—and I do mean *dig*. Ponder, process, and answer. Often, writing down your thoughts helps create the best outcome.

I strongly encourage you to keep a journal and be generous with the time you spend recording your thoughts. Typing on a device is fine, but the act of moving your hand to write while thinking can produce significant insights that may be missed while keyboarding.

WHY SHOULD I TAKE TIME FOR A PERSONAL RETREAT AND WHAT MIGHT IMPEDE MY SUCCESS?

A personal retreat is meant to help *you* design *your* life. Instead of allowing life to happen to you as a result of serendipitous opportunities and random setbacks, choose to take charge. Most people take a break from their daily routine by taking a vacation or relaxing at home. The difference between these casual interludes and a personal retreat is the element of intent. A personal retreat is a conscious effort to feed your mind, body, and spirit what it needs to thrive.

You may encounter challenges as you attempt to plan and execute your personal retreat. Below are a few of the obstacles you may encounter, but by recognizing them and being prepared to deal with them, you'll find a way forward.

Letting Time Slip By

It can be challenging to find the balance between relaxation and adherence to an agenda that serves your purpose. I've gone on many retreats where the environment is so relaxing that I daze and doze the day away. If my intention is simply to relax and unwind, then this is great. However, if I have a more specific goal, such as finding ways to regain balance in my life, sleeping and watching the clouds float by may not provide the results I'm seeking.

Safety

Choose a location where you feel comfortable. I have a friend who likes to camp alone in the middle of nowhere without another human being for miles! Although that's rewarding for her, I would spend my whole time in fear of bears, bugs, and lack of cell phone coverage.

Emotional Distress

Depending on your retreat focus and your unique personal circumstances, some retreats can be more emotional than others. If you ever have a time when your feelings overwhelm you during your discovery phase, it is important to have a special person to call if you cannot guide yourself back to a healthy place.

Expecting Too Much of Yourself

Your intention may be derailed by a new thought that occurs during your retreat. Don't assume you've failed if your intention is transformed by your experience. Allow yourself to travel down any path that presents itself. Allow yourself to go where your thoughts take you. Unexpected sparks of insight may occur.

QUICK START PREPARATION GUIDE

Plan ahead for your personal retreat, setting aside time for it on your calendar. Avoid conflicts and obstacles in advance. For example:

- If you plan your *personal retreat at home*, clean the house the day before so you are not distracted.

- If you plan your *personal retreat away*, research offsite locations in advance. Check hours of operation, directions, fees, and the resources needed to meet the goal of your personal retreat.

- If you plan an *outdoor personal retreat*, have a backup plan in case of bad weather.

- Don't plan your *personal retreat* in the middle of a busy week. Choose a day when clock watching will be unnecessary or at least minimal.

- Warn family and friends that you can only be reached for important matters.

GATHER THE THINGS YOU'LL NEED

Here is a list of suggested items you might like to have available during your personal retreat. Only you will know which ones will enable you to fulfill your objective:

- A journal or a notebook, pens, and pencils.

- Stationery to write letters or paper to draw on. A large flip chart and markers might also be helpful.

- Books, special photos, or mementos that might stimulate thought relevant to your objective.

- Music for dancing or meditation.

- A camera.

- A timer.

- Candles (don't forget the matches!).

- Clothes that fit your location and mood.

- Choose or prepare food aligned with your objective; it could be cleansing or healthful, or deliciously decadent.

- Surround yourself with a fragrance that is meaningful to you. It could be incense, essential oils, or maybe even hand lotion.

- And finally, if appropriate for your personal retreat location, bring items to pamper yourself, such as bubble bath and manicure/pedicure essentials.

SHOULD A RETREAT BE STRUCTURED OR UNSTRUCTURED?

If you are new to personal retreats, please strongly consider creating an agenda for yourself as part of your pre-event planning. While I believe that unstructured retreats have significant value, an inexperienced retreater may find distraction the enemy of intention. On the flipside, there is no rule that says you have to follow an agenda minute by minute, either. Let yourself go—both mentally and physically—and let the moment have its say.

Retreat experts agree that having an agenda prevents you from getting to the personal retreat location and then saying, "Now what?" A person who spends all their time trying to figure out why they are on a personal retreat in the first place may leave their retreat wondering what the big deal was. Remember, an agenda is just a manifestation of your intention, and intention is something you should have in hand before you begin your retreat.

A *Sample Agenda for a One-Day Retreat* is offered at the end of the book. It can be modified to fit the amount of time you've chosen for your personal retreat, and used again and again.

CREATE A "NEST" FOR YOUR PERSONAL RETREAT

Now that you've chosen an appropriate location, gather all of the items you think you may need and place them within reach so you won't have to interrupt your focus by getting up and down. Find the most comfortable position in which to read, relax, and think. Be conscious of your comfort level and move around as often as you like to keep your body in a happy place.

If you don't have a deadline, consider removing all clocks and allowing yourself the luxury of not caring about time. Take telephones off the hook and turn off your cell too!

Opening Ceremony

Starting your personal retreat with an *opening ceremony* simply helps you focus your heart and mind and drown out distraction. The nest you create should match your intention and the time you've allotted. It should invite you to withdraw and enter your special space...and begin.

Your commitment to releasing and replacing everyday concerns with sharp intention is vitally important. For many first-time retreaters, this may feel awkward, but I encourage you to persevere until you succeed. As you become more comfortable in your personal retreat setting, you'll find unique ways to maintain your focus. Release a distraction by identifying it, and then attempting to suppress the thought to the back of your mind.

An opening ceremony is deeply personal and generally utilizes music, rhythm, objects, or symbolic gestures. These elements allow you to build a bridge between your inner self and your intention. There are no rules for an opening ceremony and no one can judge what is appropriate for you. Explore techniques until you find what works. Your goal is to be *totally present* in the moment.

My first personal retreat, over two decades ago, occurred on a beautiful spring day in a local park. I had my thermos of tea, a self-help book, and plenty of paper. I jumped right into my *reading* and *processing*, and before I knew it, I was distracted by all kinds of unfocused thoughts that were not advantageous in reaching my goal. The only thing I really succeeded in doing that day was reading in the park for an afternoon. While this was very pleasant, it was not quite the day I had imagined.

By the same time the following year, I'd attended a women's retreat where I received many great ideas from other people who had more experience with personal retreats, which enabled me to put more thought into the start of my special day. This time, I chose my home as my personal retreat location. I knew months in advance about a weekend in July when my husband and children would be gone overnight. "What a great opportunity for a personal retreat at home," I thought. Although it felt awkward at first, I created an opening ceremony based on what I had recently learned. I gathered the supplies I would need: candles, matches, music, a new set of markers, and flip-chart paper. I turned off all phones and located my favorite selection of quiet music. As the first song played, I closed my eyes and inhaled slowly and deeply. I exhaled slowly and relaxed my shoulders until I felt peaceful. After repeating this exercise several times, I opened my eyes and lit a candle. I concentrated on the flicker of the flame and attempted to keep my mind as blank as possible. The music continued to play and I felt the tension I held escape. Having no timetable for the next two days, I allowed myself to just be. Finally, when the time felt right, I read these words out loud as if talking to a trusted friend:

"My energy is focused on just this one task. All other distractions are gone. Life outside continues without me for just this personal retreat.

I'm in a bubble that is safe, comforting, and complete.
I love it here. Today I will ask myself the following question..."

Then, I opened my new markers and began writing down my thoughts and drawing pictures. It was during this dedicated moment in time that the purest and most insightful flashes of wisdom occurred. My entire opening ceremony lasted only fifteen minutes, but when I was done, I felt calm, with laser-focused energy like no other. I was ready to begin.

The creative options for an opening ceremony are unlimited. Sharon Wesolowski, a inner wisdom guide from Portland, Oregon, uses nature to get started:

My opening ceremony was structured around a walk to the beach. I meditated prior to setting out and simply asked that I remain open to what the ocean, sand, and waves wished to teach me. While on the beach I was inspired to gather little treasures: rocks, shells, driftwood, feathers, seaweed, beach grass, etc. I walked slowly, ran with my dog, paused often to listen and look above, below, and around. I felt in the flow of what was arising during this opening, settling, and centering time. When I returned to the house, I began to create little driftwood assemblages that reflected and were filled with the love and unique inner gifts I had received from each of my immediate family. The creative process helped me let go of false perceptions that anyone else or mothering/family life were holding me back from engaging deeply with my life passions. As I brought the driftwood creations together, I felt an inner reclaiming of how my heart wished to express itself and with each piece, a story came through and a title was created. I gave these beach sculptures to my husband and two sons that Christmas.

Here are some other examples of opening ceremonies. They are simple personal retreat *fire starters*:

- A centering walk like the one Sharon Wesolowksi related is common and very helpful. Recite your personal retreat intention to help you focus.

- If you're driving to your personal retreat location, use your car ride as part of your opening ceremony. Play specific music. Drive a certain route. Breathe deeply at every stopping point or sing at the top of your lungs.

- If you wish to release anger, grief, or conflict, consider a cleansing activity such as safely burning objects in a fireplace or engaging in high-energy dancing to music that matches your intention.

- Exercise is another favorite opening ceremony for many people. Yoga, running, swimming, and working out are all great ways to get the blood pumping and the brain focused.

- Some people pray and others meditate.

Finally, it is important that the amount of time you spend on your opening ceremony is proportionate to the overall length of your retreat. In other words, if you are planning a mini-retreat lasting only a few hours, it is best to keep your opening time short and sweet. Move toward your intention and your inner work in a timely manner. If the fun of an opening ceremony takes on a life of its own, your allotted time will be gone before you realize it. You may want to create a short and simple opening ceremony that you repeat every time, thereby taking away the pressure to be creative or think up something new. Remember, the objective is to get your mind and heart ready to explore. Whatever way you accomplish this level of mindfulness is fine. It may just require a few deep breaths to be good to go. Conversely, if you are retreating for a weekend or longer, a bigger block of time can be dedicated to your opening ceremony.

After years of conducting my own retreats, I have developed several concepts that work well for my personality. What I have found most important is to allow myself to think, speak out loud, and move in that moment, without inhibition.

There is great freedom in being who you are.

Self-Reflective Reading
& Responding

Solving a Problem & Making Decisions

"The degree of our
discontent is
directly related to
the gap between our
intentions and
our conduct."

~Michelle DeAngelis
Author of *Get a Life That Doesn't Suck*

How Do I Figure Things Out?
Sorting Through Options

Have you ever had a moment that changed the course of your life? My moment occurred on January 26, 2000. I was giving a presentation at the American Club in Kohler, Wisconsin. They were hosting a women's wellness retreat and I was invited to join. Little did I know what an impact that event would have on my life.

They offered a session titled, "Sorting It Out." A woman by the name of Priscilla Dean offered the opportunity to meet with her for thirty minutes at the cost of $30 to talk about anything you wanted to "sort out." I thought it might be an interesting opportunity to figure out an issue I'd had on my mind for a while. My dilemma revolved around a decision, whether or not to leave my current employer and try to earn a living as a professional speaker. Priscilla seemed like a person I'd feel comfortable talking to, so I went.

We met in a small conference room. After I shared my challenge, she thrust a diagram in front of me. The piece of paper had a sunburst in the middle of the page. She prompted me to list all factors influencing my decision to abandon my career. She instructed me to put one entry on each ray of the sunburst. Without hesitation, I quickly filled in the first four lines: salary concerns, obligation to present employer, family opinion, and uncertainty of success in a new field.

After coming up with the easy four, I reclined slightly in my folding chair and contemplated the other five blank lines on the page. I clearly remember questioning her, "Am I only supposed to write down the things tipping me toward *no*?"

She said, "Of course not. Include everything that is influencing your decision." With a burst of excitement, I was able to finish the circle, adding many factors that pointed toward the answer, *yes*, leave the job.

That's it—only nine influencing factors to "sort through" and I'd have my answer. We discussed each of my entries, giving complete focus to one factor at a time. The first thing she pointed out was the importance I placed on the input of others. Sorting through all the facts, I realized I was so caught up in not disappointing or going against their opinions that I'd turned the need for permission into one of the major hurdles affecting my decision. Priscilla challenged me to consider the worst thing that could happen if I went against the advice of others. I could not come up with anything other than, "They would disagree and try to talk me out of it." My sorting-it-out coach urged me to walk out of our session with an "I am" statement regarding my career path intention: "I am going to quit my job and start my own company." I had trouble agreeing to this challenge, but I finally accepted it. I'd found the nerve to verbalize it. There was no turning back. Turns out, what I thought was my biggest hurdle wasn't that big after all. The people in my life, whose support I needed, stood behind me all the way. In sharing this story with others, I've learned that the opinions of others have great influence on us and can create some of our biggest stumbling blocks when we're struggling with personal choices.

Next, Priscilla asked me about my uncertainty of success in my new career: "Do you think you could make it in the speaking field?"

I said, "Without a doubt, I can do this." I had never said those words out loud to anyone, but I knew in my heart it was true. Aside from being the mother to my children, I can honestly say that professional speaking is what I was meant to do in this world.

We spent the remainder of the session dissecting the rest of the influences. Untangling the details of each entry on the diagram was enjoyable. When I left that room, I had made up my mind to take action and pursue my dream. I promised myself: "I will make a sensible plan to quit my job and speak for a living. I am going to do everything in my power to live the life that was meant for me. No one can do that for me."

When I realized I had taken more time with the coach than my initial investment would cover, I offered to pay the difference. I will *never* forget Priscilla's reply, "You know how you can pay me? JUST—GO—DO." What an amazing statement. Stop talking; start doing.

Now it's your turn to JUST—GO—DO.

_____ a s k   y o u r s e l f . . .

What's on my mind and in my heart that needs sorting out?

Take the time to complete the Sunburst Sort Out found at the end
of this section.

Review the concerns or challenges you've written on each ray; focus
on them one at a time and reflect on the following:

What is the worst that can happen?

What is the best that can happen?

What needs to change for me to JUST — GO — DO?

What is my calling at this time of my life?

What specific action(s) invite me to the happiest life possible over the
next twelve months?

Finish this exercise with an "I am" statement and say it out loud.

"I am _____
."

thoughts...

"In order to move
forward, I must learn
the difference between
giving up and letting go."

~Jen Hannah
Songwriter & Singer

Finding Closure

Is anyone good with good-byes? In 2006, my parents made the decision to sell the family farm and retire. It wasn't a decision that came overnight. My great-grandfather had purchased the land in 1913 and raised seven children there. My father was the last child born at the farm, and the only son. I was raised on the same land and spent my entire childhood in the house my grandfather had built when my dad was nine. I loved my home, and although I never planned on moving back there as an adult, it never dawned on me that I might not have the option. I was shocked when my folks shared their intention to quit farming and sell the homestead. My selfish side yearned to convince them to wait. Instead, I chose to support their choice unconditionally, as did every other member of our close-knit family.

In preparation for the estate sale, we purged the cobwebbed attic and the faded old barn. For us it was a trip down memory lane, but Mom was simply looking to get the job done and her mantra became, "Pitch it. Burn it." I was surprised by my reluctance to trash certain possessions. For instance, my mother's 1936 first-edition Monopoly set, which had been used to teach me the game. The board is now yellowed with age and the bills are rice-paper thin from years of exchanging hands. The wooden houses and hotels are barely recognizable. Mom told me she and I used to argue over who was going to get the iron as a playing piece. She thought I only wanted it because I knew it was her favorite piece. I have no memory of that, but I do know that today I wouldn't fight over an iron in any situation. Now, when I remove the box lid, the musty smell sends me back home to the attic of the farmhouse I loved.

Another item I rescued from the farm was an old wingback chair my parents purchased as newlyweds. The large floral pattern of brown, orange, and yellow was proof of its 1950s origin. Dad tells the story of how he wrote a check for it, but because they were shopping out of the area, the clerk was hesitant to take it. A neighbor happened to be in the store at the same time, and she also knew the clerk. She said, "I can vouch for him. That check is good." My dad was proud when he told that story because he is known as a man of his word and has always been someone a neighbor would vouch for. I hauled that chair home and had it reupholstered to match my office. I look at it every day as a reminder of his integrity and aspire to be a person others will vouch for.

The sale of the farm could not have gone better. A wonderful family with two small children bought the place. I've never met them, but I hear the kids are discovering the little hiding places I had as a child, like the hideaway fort under the stairs leading to the second floor. It has a tiny door, and inside there are three shelves, two hooks, and pencil marks measuring the height of my favorite doll, Puddins. There is just enough room in the nook to host a tea party for two, with room for each to bring an imaginary friend. Even though I knew a great family was taking ownership, it didn't make my final trip down the eighth-of-a-mile lane any easier. I've never been good with final moments or goodbyes. I'm embarrassed to say I tear up at the end of almost every movie and occasionally even a commercial. I expected my folks to be broken up during the final days of their homestead's ownership. But I was wrong. They were calm, methodical, focused. I commented to Dad about this and he said, "Hey, you gotta keep looking forward. You can't look behind you." I thought, *I hope I can be that strong and focused when I reach my parents' stage of life.* Then, I realized that possessing strength and focus applies during all stages of our lives. It's the awareness you have when a new era begins and you are at peace with the era that has passed. This quality, in itself, is an accomplishment.

Moving forward means you're living.
That alone is a celebration.

ask yourself...

What goodbyes do I need to prepare for?

What closure do I need in order to prepare for something new?

Has a door been closed that I wasn't ready to close? What do I want to do about that?

If I want it reopened, am I the one to make the first move?

"Lasting change happens when
we pull back the layers
and get to the root
of the problem. Then we
can make conscious choices
towards the greater good."

~Bonnie Artman Fox
Speaker & Coach

How Can I Change?
Create an Opposite Plan

It was a cloudy, dreary day. So, as I pulled out of the garage, I decided to run back inside and grab an umbrella even though I was uncertain of showers. As I climbed back into the car, my seven-year-old daughter Ellie said, "We don't always *know* when it's going to rain, that's for sure."

Profound words from a wise child. True, we don't always know when it's going to rain, but we do know *it will,* sooner or later. It even rains in the Sahara Desert. Sure, only an average of three inches a year falls, but it does rain. Growing up a farmer's daughter in the Midwest, I know all about the importance of rain. Our income was dependent upon the amount of rain that fell each year. Too much rain and there would be a flood; too little rain and there would be a drought. Just the right amount of precipitation would bring a bumper crop for all and a drop in the price per bushel. My father always said he didn't need to spend time in a casino because he was a professional gambler by occupation.

One year, we had a particularly dry season in our area. Every day, the farmers prayed for rain. That same summer, I had a coworker planning an outdoor wedding. She was asking everyone to pray it *wouldn't* rain. I was struck by the deep desire both she and my father had regarding rain, yet it was the opposite prayer. Well, both had their prayers answered because on the day of her wedding, the two o'clock ceremony was completed underneath a beautiful, sunny sky. By five o'clock, the indoor reception had started and only then did the clouds open up and drop a steady rain most of the night, providing a fantastic ground soak. That Sunday morning, both the bride and farmer woke up happy.

That may sound like the punch line of a bad joke, but my point is that many moments hinge on one turn of an event. It is the *being prepared* part that helps give us a sense of control. My coworker was so certain it wasn't going to rain that day that she didn't have a backup plan. My father, on the other hand, always worked extra jobs and had savings in case the weather didn't work out as he hoped. Granted, her issue was with a one-day event, not livelihood, but the mindset is what I'd like you to think about. Are you the confident "It won't happen to me" type or are you a "What's my plan if it doesn't work out the way I prayed" type? What's the one thing on your mind today that you are counting on to go smoothly, exactly as planned? Now imagine the opposite happens. Are the consequences of the opposite too big to handle? Do you have a backup plan that will work?

On several occasions, I have busted out of a place of discontent by actively trying to do the opposite of my normal behavior. If you currently find yourself wishing for a change, but are not sure how to get there, try this exercise.

List the negative aspects of your life in one-word entries. For example:

TIRED
CONFUSED
SAD
OVERWHELMED
LONELY

Establish space for a second column, but leave it blank for now. In the third column, write the opposite of the words in column one.

TIRED	*	AWAKE
CONFUSED	*	CLEAR-MINDED
SAD	*	HAPPY
OVERWHELMED	*	CALM
LONELY	*	CONNECTED

Now, go back to the middle column and indicate the specific action you need to take to make the opposite happen. When you're done, the grid will look something like this:

TIRED	GET MORE REST/EXERCISE	AWAKE
CONFUSED	MAKE DECISIONS	CLEAR-MINDED
SAD	LAUGH	HAPPY
OVERWHELMED	GET THINGS DONE	CALM
LONELY	CALL SOMEONE	CONNECTED

The last step in this exercise is to create a behavior list using the actions in the middle column. Work to be as specific as you can with your action steps. For example, if the first action is to get more rest and exercise, your behavior list would say something like:

✓ Start going to bed one hour earlier.

✓ Stop watching TV after dinner and relax or read to calm my mind.

✓ Walk thirty minutes daily or join a workout group.

Don't limit your ideas by saying "can't" or "don't know how."
Instead, say, "In what way can I accomplish this goal?"

————————————————————————— a s k y o u r s e l f...

How much control and/or influence do I have over what feels
negative in my life?

Can I be even more honest with myself about my responsibility to
change what bugs me?

What do I need to do now to initiate meaningful change?

_____ thoughts...

"There doesn't have to be
anyone who understands you.
There just has to be someone
who wants to."

~Robert Brault
American Writer

Mindset for Dealing with Change and Stress

During a downturn in our economy, I was told the story of a local restaurant owner who was nervous about the possible decline in business. He didn't want to change the quality or quantity of his food and he certainly couldn't raise prices. Instead of behaving as if his fate was out of his control, he chose to become involved in the things he *could* control. When he started reviewing the orders from suppliers, he found waste. The more he dug into the outflow of cash, the more he learned about the health of his business. He found changes that should have been made long ago even without an economic crisis. His attitude changed as if a reset button had been pushed and he began to monitor a basic business function—*owner control of spending*—with more care. He is now upbeat about the health of his business. I heard this story from one of his friends while attending an event at his restaurant. The place was full of people eating, drinking, and spending money. The owner smiled and greeted me warmly. He definitely had the look of a man whose system was running smoothly.

Creating a mindset to deal with change is far from easy. We all know that change is constant, but being advised to "just deal with it" doesn't help very much. I've always appreciated coaching that comes in the form of a recommended action. This inspired me to develop an exercise I often present during one of my speeches that guides others to take control of what they can, and accept what they cannot. Yes, that sounds like a slice of the Serenity Prayer written in the 1940s, but its worth is timeless. One thing remains consistent throughout time—change.

There are generally three levels of resistance to change. Low resistance occurs when things can be changed back with minimal effort or expense. For example, rearranging your living room furniture or accepting a lunch invitation with a new friend doesn't take much decision making, nor will you encounter much stress in the action.

The next stage comes with moderate resistance. This type of action does not represent a permanent change, but it seems risky at the time. Deciding to relocate or breaking off a struggling relationship is a much more difficult change to make and is usually not taken lightly.

Finally, stage three of change often has lots of resistance because it requires a new way of thinking and behaving and is difficult to reverse, maybe even impossible. It can involve a deep personal change of some kind, like converting religions or deciding to start a family. This type of change takes time and an evaluation of all options before confidently moving forward.

Why do people resist change and what holds them back? Fear of the unknown, complacency, previous knowledge and experience can all play a part. Often, our own limiting factors can be at work in the form of a voice in our heads that talks negatively and splashes doubt. Finding balance during stressful times can help manage the mental anguish of change.

Let me offer examples of how to cope with the three levels of change, that is: no control, some control, and complete control.

NO CONTROL

Off the top of your head, think of a situation in your life right now that may be causing you stress, over which you have absolutely *no control*. Do you think you have been dwelling on it recently? A common example that pops up when I go through this exercise with an audience is the stress caused by our economy and the fear of losing a job. Often, people feel they have absolutely no control over this situation. It has been the topic of every newscast and is impossible to ignore. I have a friend who copes with this by not reading a newspaper or listening to the news because of the negative energy it brings into her life. I am not advocating this approach, but for her, it works. She does not dwell on the financial crisis of our country one bit!

SOME CONTROL

Next, think of a situation in your life right now that may be causing you stress, over which you have *some control*. Most often, this stressor involves other people or struggling relationships. The challenge of this dilemma is to accurately assess your role in the circumstance and take responsibility where appropriate. The tug-o-war of who did what to whom and how it affects "me" is an important part. When an attendee at a speech volunteers to share on this point, she often describes a difficult relationship, whether that be professional or personal. Frequently the attendee will share feelings of being wronged by the other person. When I softly push back and ask her to focus only on the part that is within her control, the shift happens. Sometimes there is a flash of realization that she can do more to relieve her own stress. She gets more upset with the lack of control she perceives. We have better luck finding resolutions if the focus remains on action within our control. We make progress in dealing with change when I ask, sometimes repeatedly, "What is it that you *can* do that would make this situation better?"

COMPLETE CONTROL

Finally, think of a situation in your life right now that may be causing you stress, over which you have *complete control*. One of my greatest self-inflicted stressors is crowding my calendar with too many commitments. I like to do a variety of things and I rarely say no to an invitation, so it is not uncommon for my calendar to run me ragged. Then, when I complain about stress, I have to stop and take complete responsibility for my situation. Throughout this book you will read several examples of how I created themes around taking control of my schedule. It has been one the greatest things I have done for myself. I am confident that if your stress meter is off the charts, the first place to start is by managing the number of entries on your calendar with a stronger hand.

When things are balanced, we can handle the stress that comes with our activities of daily living or ADLs. I don't believe it is possible to be completely free of stress within a normal lifestyle. In fact, many believe that "good stress" is what drives us to take positive and productive actions in our lives. Consider taking the time now to complete Exercise #3, the Stress Processor, found at the end of this section.

Taking action is the best way to create a positive change mindset and handle the stress associated with it.

_____ a s k   y o u r s e l f . . .

On a scale of 1–10, with 10 being high, what is my current stress level?

If it is 5 or less, ask yourself, "What have I done to achieve this acceptable level?"

If it is 6 or higher, "Am I interested in taking charge of lowering this number?"

If you answered "Yes" to the previous question, see the stress exercise in this chapter.

"I don't regret the things
I've done, I regret the
things I didn't do when
I had the chance."

~Anonymous~

Taking a "GUTSY" Approach to Creating the Life You Want

For years, my most popular keynote speech was titled, "20 Ideas That Can Change Your Life." I ended up renaming it because audience members routinely shared afterward that what they were looking for were *big ideas* on how to effect change. They wanted ideas that would revolutionize the life they were currently living. Although not one of them ever gave me an example of the concept they were seeking, I imagined radical actions like quitting a job, leaving a spouse, or traveling around the world. My twenty ideas were not as dramatic and it led me to ponder the idea of how one actively creates a desirable life.

I admire people who are *gutsy* about their life. Take charge, take action—these are the philosophies of those who know how to get it done. I asked myself,

> *What are the action steps the "gutsy" people use*
> *to create the life they want?*

G = GET FOCUSED

You may know a famous line from the movie, *The Shining*: "All work and no play makes Jack a dull boy." Well, all talk and no action also makes Jack a dumb boy. I've been guilty of this and likely, so have you. Are you constantly talking about what you are going to do without ever moving one step closer to actually doing it? A personal retreat is a great time to remove all distractions and focus on just one aspect of your life that needs direction. Being focused is a critical component of the success of the *gutsy* crew.

U = USE ALL RESOURCES

There are bound to be untapped resources within the people you know. Brilliant solutions to challenges you face are quite possibly found in the minds of your inner tribe or their circle of influence. Who can you interview for help? Ask: What books can you research? Where can you go to learn more or to absorb good vibes in a particular environment?

T = TAKE A CHANCE

I made a mental list of the people I think have been *gutsy* when making their life choices. Although they have a variety of qualities that are similar, the one common denominator is their strength and willingness to take a chance. They weren't afraid to fail. They took responsibility for their own choices. They weren't satisfied with good enough. They were always looking for better and smarter ways to get things done. They have a fire in their spirit that can't be put out, no matter how hard critics try to extinguish it.

S = START AND STOP

Simply fill in the blanks below. I say "simply" tongue-in-cheek, because when you really dive into this exercise, it's as far away from simple as you can get.

To create the life I want...

I must start _____ and stop _____.

Y = YEARLY REVIEW

Successful organizations review their business plan yearly. Run your life like the flourishing company you know it can be. As the CEO of your world, it is important to formally "check-in" with a yearly review of your life. A textbook example of how to create a business plan fits well with a life plan too. The classic SWOT analysis, when applied to your life, takes on a whole new meaning. Reviewing your **S**trengths, **W**eaknesses, **O**pportunities, and **T**hreats to your happiness is a good place to start. From there, you can develop future goals, check your financial stability, and even create a personal board of directors. Several of my self-employed friends have created a "personal board of directors" and found it helpful. A few times a year they gather a selection of people who influence them to toss around ideas or challenges facing them both personally and professionally. One friend in particular relies on her board to give her honest, blunt feedback when she is contemplating a new idea.

As I've told you, *gutsy* is a word that fires me up. Just looking it up in the thesaurus motivates me to be bolder when I make decisions. Deeply digest the following words and see if one or all of them do the same for you:

Assertive • Audacious • Bold • Brazen • Certain • Confident

Courageous • Determined • Gallant • Gung ho • Resolute

Spirited • Spunky • Unflappable • Valiant

Many people report they are attracted to those who are confident. If this is not your strength, consider spending some time making a decision on how to move one small step in the *gutsy* direction.

I do believe that GUTSY can change your life.

_____ ask yourself...

What do I need to focus on now to create the life I want?

What are the resources I need to accomplish my greatest attainable desire?

Am I ready to take a chance?

How do I finish the start and stop question in this chapter?

Who would I ask to be on my personal board of directors and why?

thoughts...

Exercise

no.1

The Sunburst Sort-Out

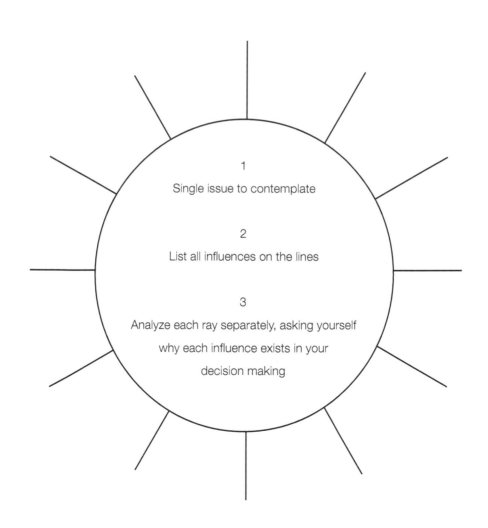

1

Single issue to contemplate

2

List all influences on the lines

3

Analyze each ray separately, asking yourself

why each influence exists in your

decision making

Exercise
no.2

Quick Take

"In quickness, there is truth," is a famous quote from author Ray Bradbury. I wasn't sure I understood what he meant until I tried this exercise. Set a timer for fifteen minutes and write nonstop about a particular topic. Suggested topics may include:

- What is really bothering you?

- Where do you want to be in ten years?

- Who are the people you are grateful for, and why?

- If you knew your life was nearing its end, what would you be sad to have never done?

Don't concern yourself with penmanship, spelling, grammar, or neatness. Don't take time to ponder or mentally search for the right words. Just allow your subconscious mind to come to the surface. It is important you don't sensor yourself while doing this exercise. Remember, you can always destroy the end result!

When I did this exercise years ago, some important personal thoughts came to me. I didn't analyze my writing as I am usually inclined to do. Instead, I folded the large flip chart piece of paper into a small square and I put it away. I didn't read it again until almost a year later and I was surprised at some of the things I had recorded that I didn't even remember writing. That was over ten years ago, and I still pull it out on occasion to review it. When I say the words out loud, I am emotionally transported back to the day it was written. I realize many of the actions I have taken in the last ten years are directly connected to that quick-take exercise.

Exercise

no.3

Stress Processor

Make a list of the things currently causing your stress. Try not to analyze as you write them down; simply jot each on paper and move on to the next entry. When you are done, divide them into one of three categories.

1.   Things you have *no* control over

2.   Things you have *some* control over

3.   Things you have *complete* control over

For the entries you feel you have *no control* over, apply the *process of diversion*. This means, find an action that decreases dwelling upon the stressor. For example, I worked with a woman whose mother was dying. It was obviously out of my friend's control and deep stress was associated with dwelling on the terminal disease for months. When we discussed a diversion, she was, at first, unable to think of one. Then it occurred to her that her mother used to love to read but was no longer healthy enough. My friend picked up a selection of mysteries and started reading to her mother when she visited. They found that the time spent dwelling on the illness decreased. It didn't make all the stress go away, but it sure did help.

For the entries you feel you have *some control* over, apply the process of *direct change of conduct*. Instead of wishing the other person would make the first move, you move. Instead of complaining about the behavior of others, take positive action and change your own conduct. For example, a doctor at one of my programs shared that his office staff were very disrespectful and childish at times. He felt a great deal of stress surrounding their lack of professionalism and all logical training attempts and discipline had fallen short. When I asked what direct action he could take, he was defensive. After much consideration, he decided he could stop yelling at them and instead approach them with a positive, fresh start. He made a plan, executed it, and later reported progress had been made.

For the entries that you feel you have *complete control* over, apply the process of *do*! The first time you try this exercise for yourself, you may be amazed at the number of stressors that you can process right off the list by just simply *doing*! A perfect example many of you may relate to is the stress resulting from clutter around the house. I have great intentions but something else is always grabbing my attention and my labor. Yet, when I take the time to focus on my own stressors, some version of "clutter" is *always* on the list. It feels so good to *do* and cross it off.

Remember, the goal is to process stress by taking the action described in each situation below.

No Control = Look for a diversion.

Some Control = Change your conduct.

Complete Control = Do and cross it off the list!

Self-Improvement &
Personal Processing

"It's a helluva start,
being able to
recognize what makes
you happy."

~Lucille Ball
Legendary Actress
1911-1989

What Does Happy Look Like?

Are you ready to unleash your genie from its bottle? After writing the first chapter of this book on the topic of sorting things out, I started thinking about Priscilla Dean, the woman responsible for the session that changed the course of my life many years ago. I decided to track her down. It was a challenge to find her since she had moved away from Wisconsin ages ago. So, I played amateur private detective and tracked her down on the Internet. It took several attempts, but I finally found her and she had a pretty good memory of me all these years later. I shared my chapter with her and asked if she would be willing to add her thoughts to my book. She has hosted many sessions with people trying to "sort things out" and I was certain she would have an interesting insight. This is the beautiful response I received from her not long after my request:

> "Sorting it out" starts with perceptive listening and asking the right questions. Most people know in their hearts what they are capable of. When that does not surface easily, a need for approval is usually attached to the stopper that holds the genie in the bottle. If we take a look at what approval is needed, it will likely lead us to the right question.

> We can shake down our parents, siblings, environment, heredity, and most assuredly, they all have a part in it. Then the question that we must ask ourselves is, "Why does it matter?" Aha, we come to self—self-confidence, opinion of self, view of self. Next question

is, "Who cares?" We have one life to live. If we allow anyone or anything to prevent us from being our fullest, shame on us. Stating something so simply and as matter of fact may ring hollow in your ears. If you have a passion for something, then you are ahead of the game because it is already clear to you what you want to do. If you have an uneasy feeling, an unrest, then the passion or the need has not been able to surface. I would like to offer a suggestion, a place to start. Something that is good for all of us to review periodically. I have developed a worksheet on "what makes us happy."

For five days in a row, make a list of the things that make you happy. It's okay to repeat things from a previous day. Each day start a NEW sheet and do NOT look at what you wrote the day before. Keep all the pages. (However, if you are only on a one-day retreat, go ahead and make the list and go straight to the questions.)

HAPPY INVENTORY

After you have completed five days of listing what makes you happy, reflect on the following questions:

1. Do I do these things now?
2. Do I do this with others?
3. Does this cost money?
4. How much time does it require?
5. What time of day do I do this?
6. How can I bring this into my weekly schedule? Daily life?
7. What are the similarities and differences of my happy inventory?
8. What strikes me most about this list?
9. How does it make me feel?

Priscilla finished her letter by sharing:

I vowed I would never write a book on gardening because every year gardening is different. However, every year my garden teaches me something. One thing I have learned is that no matter what the weather hands out, something thrives. What does that mean to you? Maybe something/someone out there is waiting for what you have to offer. Waiting for that song, that sentence, that smile, that encouragement, that recipe. Finding out what makes us happy is a good start in knowing our heart's wish.

I did Pricilla's exercise just as instructed. Surprisingly, I ended up with thirteen different entries on my five-day list. What grabbed my attention was the fact that almost half of the things I said "make me happy" are things controlled by others. Discovering this fact changed how I behave. I noticed that I waited for others to bring me the happy. My previous formula was:

$$S + O = H \text{ (SITUATION + OTHERS = HAPPY)}$$

As a result, I created a plan where my happiness equation had to include a "me" symbol. I changed it to:

$$M + A = H \text{ (ME + ACTION = HAPPY)}$$

Make yourself happy. A good friend of mind did the Happy Inventory and realized making time to drink tea in her backyard made her happy. The appearance of her yard did not. So, as soon as her budget allowed, she did a complete overhaul of her garden. It is now a place of tranquility and a perfect garden of happiness for her and all who visit. This is a great example of someone making a bubble of happy for herself.

Thank you, Priscilla, for taking time to write for my book. I only spent one hour of my life with you, but it was profound. You let my genie out of its bottle and she has been dancing ever since.

"Someone out there
is waiting for what you have to offer.
Waiting for that song, that sentence, that smile,
that encouragement, that recipe."

Priscilla Dean
Sort-It-Out Leader

_____ ask yourself...

What is the "happy" that I want for me?

What insights emerged after writing my Happiness Inventory?

Can my insights be even more specific?

"Whatever you want
to do, do it now.
There are only
so many tomorrows."

~Michael Landon,
Actor
1936–1991

Releasing Regrets: The Coulda-Woulda Sisters

When used in a sentence *could* is often followed by *but*. *Could* implies one has the ability to achieve, and that's where the honesty needs to start. "I *coulda* been an astronaut." No, I don't like science or math, therefore no space program for me, *but...*

I *coulda* been a size five, *but* bad choices worked against me. A few years ago, I went to see my doctor, and with a serious tone, he asked, "How is it possible that a *motivational speaker* can have a weight problem?" I thought about it for a second and then replied, "That's easy. When I see the Golden Arches, I'm motivated to turn in."

Many experts say there is a deep-seated reason that overeaters struggle; traumatic childhood, low self-esteem, etc. None of their suspected reasons apply to me. I had a fabulous childhood, no traumas, no grief. I have a loving, fully intact family; my world is good. Then I heard about repression. It's not uncommon for people who have faced severe abuse to block it out. I wish you could have seen my mother's face the day I asked her to be straight with me and tell me if I'd been beaten or locked in a closet when I was little. For the record, the answer is, "no," and I think it's possible I offended her a little by asking. So, if my problem isn't due to trauma or abuse, what is the reason? Simple: I love food. There's a shocker. If I loved booze, I'd be a drinker. If I loved gambling, I'd be in debt. And if I loved space, I'd be an astronaut.

Is there something on your mind that you feel you *coulda* done *but* didn't? What is the specific reason you didn't?

Coulda implies time has passed you by and there's no going back. Is that really true in your answers above? Could you do it now or do you think it's too late? I can't tell you how many times I have heard a person say, "I always wanted to, but it's too late now."

Several years back, I met an elderly man from a small farming town in central Illinois who shared his *coulda* story:

> I dreamed of playing the piano my entire life but never had the chance. One day, I realized it wasn't too late to chase my dream. So, I purchased a piano and started taking lessons. Mind you, I was seventy-two at that time. I started with "Mary Had a Little Lamb" and progressed from there. Although I don't aspire to play at Carnegie Hall, I do intend to play for my wife every day for the rest of my life.

The twin sister of Coulda is a feisty gal named Woulda. They seem to go almost everywhere together and are often interchangeable. What do you wish you *woulda*?

I wish I *woulda* gone to college. Looking back, I'm not sure how I made the choice not to pursue higher education. I grew up in Somonauk, Illinois, a small town in the northern part of the state, about sixty miles west of Chicago. I don't remember asking good questions about college or aspiring to do anything for a living that required expensive tuition. When I met with the guidance counselor, as all high school freshmen are required to do, I remember her saying I could be a secretary. That sounded good. The bad part is, I found out the most important attribute for a secretary is attention to detail and organization, which happen to be my greatest weaknesses. Early on, I decided a four-year college was not in my future. By accident, I ended up with a part-time job in health care and found I had a knack for dealing with patients. Eventually, I attended a technical college for medical assisting. I went on to succeed in many challenging subjects, like x-ray physics and human physiology. That's when I realized that I was smart enough to go to college, just not astute enough to ask the right questions and make the appropriate decision when I was eighteen. Ah, the wisdom gained between eighteen and forty-something is astonishing. I have only two regrets in life so far, and not going to college is one of them. I regret missing those four years that many of my friends experienced. They had the chance to meet new people, explore a fresh place, and make a lifetime of memories.

I've shared my "wish I woulda" thoughts on many occasions. One day a friend encouraged me to quit talking about them and start fixing them. I got really excited about the idea. The very next day I was flipping channels on the TV and found author Joe Kita, who wrote a book titled *Another Shot: How I Relived My Life in Less Than a Year*. It was as if he were talking directly to me from the big box in my family room. When Joe Kita turned forty, he had a midlife crisis. But instead of buying a sports car, he took a look at the biggest regrets in life and decided to do something about them. So, he tried out for his high-school basketball team, looked up his college crush, and even learned how to surf. He humorously, yet insightfully, tells how each of us can learn from our past and take advantage of the present throughout our lives.

Motivated by his words, I registered for college at forty-two with the plan of taking one class at a time until I replaced a regret with a degree. My advisor recommended I take the hardest course first. That meant the foreign language requirement. I had taken two years of French in high school but the only things I can remember are: *Quelle heure est-il?* and *Où sont les toilettes?* (What time is it? Where is the bathroom?) These sentences are probably two of the most important things to know if I ever travel to France. However, since I would be starting from scratch no matter what language I chose, Spanish seemed like the best choice. I arrived on my first day with new notebooks, pencils, and highlighters. Not surprisingly, I was the first one to class, a good ten minutes early and significantly ahead of the nineteen year olds who weren't quite as jazzed as me to be there. I still laugh when I picture the kid who slid into the desk to my left. He was wearing a black concert t-shirt from a group I've never heard of, ripped jeans, and had several piercings. He leaned over and whispered, "Hey, can I borrow a piece of paper and a pen?" I'm thinking to myself, "Who comes to class so unprepared?" I gave it to him with a motherly smile. It was unnerving to think I was likely older than his parents.

One minute before the start of the lecture, the professor bounded in with a resounding, *"Hola!"* which I figured meant hello. At first, I was proud of myself for taking a step toward fixing my regret; however, pride turned to fear when I found out that 80 percent of the class was conducted in Spanish. English would only be spoken when homework was assigned. After the first two minutes, I was lost, with no hope of keeping up. Even the kid who thought I was Office Max was keeping up. My heart dropped because I knew this wasn't the best use of my time. I'm raising a family, running a household, owning a business. "When do I have the time to make up for a twenty-year-old regret?" I asked myself. Just as the first class was wrapping up, I decided this was not necessary for me.

My college career lasted a total of fifty minutes. I was able to get a full refund for the tuition and most of the book money. The whole thing ended up costing me $50. That comes out to a buck-a-minute to get it off my mind and move on.

What I came away with was complete closure. It's true: I can get a degree at any age. I'm intelligent enough and disciplined enough to earn a diploma. However, the college experience is the part I regret missing, and nothing can give that back to me. That time is twenty-four years in the rearview mirror, and there is no reverse gear. You may read this and think it sounds like I gave up too easily. If it was such an important goal, how did I let one small challenge change my whole course of action? I don't have an answer. All I know is that three-quarters of the way through the first class, it dawned on me that by registering and showing up, I had tackled the regret. It was behind me without having to take years of classes for a degree that will not likely impact my earning ability at this stage of my career. The regret of not going to college was more sentimental than academic. Here is how I came to terms with this emotional topic. If I had gone down a different path all those years ago, life no doubt would have taken me toward different people than I share my life with today. It only takes that thought to erase a feeling of "wish I would have" from my mind.

"Wish I would have" is a fork phrase.
If you could go back to one specific moment in your life
and make a change, what moment would you change?

_____ a s k   y o u r s e l f ...

What regrets plague me?

Do I want to turn that wish into a goal and take action?

If my answer is "Yes," what is my next step?

If my answer is, "No," what can I do to release the regret I feel?

Ponder what might be different if I had taken the other path.

Replace "wish I would have" with action that results in closure.

_____ thoughts...

"Trust is like a forest.
It takes a long
time to grow and
can burn down
with just a touch
of carelessness."

~David Horsager
Bestselling author of *The Trust Edge*

Are You Getting What You Need?
And Giving It, Too?

You may remember a game made by Mattel in the late 1960s called *Tip It*. The play space was a plastic, three-legged tripod that balanced on a pole about twelve inches off the table. Each leg of the tripod held a tower of colored rings stacked in alternating order. At the very top of the tripod was a flat plastic clown balancing on his nose in a spread eagle pose. The object of the game was to remove the ring that matched your spin of the color wheel without knocking the clown off the top. As soon as the weight became significantly uneven, the tripod would tip and the clown would fall, ending the game. Although I loved the bright colored plastic pieces, I didn't love the game. I found it stressful trying to balance the clown. It seemed I was always assigned the colored ring that was the most difficult to remove. Since I was usually trying to entertain myself with this game, it wouldn't take long for me to lose interest in the balancing act and instead make up my own new game utilizing just the cool plastic parts.

Now, as an adult, I reflect back on this game and realize it is a perfect metaphor for our lives. Think of each leg of the tripod as representative of an area of your life that needs attention. Not everyone's life game looks the same, but for me, the legs represent family, work, and self. When equal attention is given to the three key areas of my life, and trust is maintained, life stays fairly balanced. But when one area is given all of my focus, my energy shifts and the other points on the tripod suffer.

I've used this metaphor many times in my programs, and one day an audience member quipped that if we only had three areas to worry about it would be much easier to balance the clown. For example, where do friends and colleagues fit on the tripod? What about attention for the mundane things in your life like maintaining your home, yard, cars, and food supply? What about making time for fun through hobbies or special interests?

The point of my *Tip It* example is congruency, the action of bringing all aspects of your life together agreeably by meeting the needs of each.

When our daughter Ellie was about four, we were having some behavior issues with her. My husband, Tom, and I were discussing this quietly at the kitchen table one evening right before bedtime. Ellie had on her Disneyworld princess pajamas that hung just about mid-thigh. She was sitting with us eating a little scoop of ice cream before bed and appeared unaware of our discussion. I said to Tom, "I recently read that when children are acting up like this, it may be because some of their needs are not being met." Ellie jumped off the chair, put her hands on her bare knees like she was about to break into a Charleston dance step and exclaimed, "Not me! My knees meet, my knees meet!"

Five years after Ellie made the knee comment, we hit a phase when my relationship with her felt off balance. I was very busy with work and a lot of my energy was spent in creative development. I love creative work and I didn't realize that multiple demands for my time were affecting her. While sharing my concerns with a colleague one day, he asked why I couldn't feed my creative needs in a way that served Ellie's needs too. *SHAZAM!* Why hadn't I thought of that? So I canceled a writing retreat I had scheduled and instead planned a mystery vacation for my daughter and me. It was a ten-day road trip through Michigan. Each night before she went to bed, she opened an envelope that told her the agenda for the next day. She scrapbooked each activity with photos and mementos we picked up along the way. We had a ball. She still talks about it from time to time. Finding a way to blend the needs of both of us made for a creative adjustment in our life.

So what *knees,* that is, needs, of others have you been missing? Take a moment to sketch out your personal *Tip It* tripod. Be as specific as you can about who and what rests on each of the pegs and don't limit yourself to three if, in fact, there are more.

Decreased balance is found in those with poor vision.
Adjust those life lenses!

_____ ask yourself...

Am I giving equal energy and focus to each leg of my tripod or base?

Are there too many legs on my base?

If yes, what can I eliminate?

Who in my life needs my focus?

Am I providing it?

What do I need from others?

Am I receiving it?

If not, have I clearly expressed my need to others?

"Creativity is allowing
yourself to make mistakes.
Art is knowing which
ones to keep."

~Scott Adams
Creator of the Dilbert Principle

Is It Time to Require
More of You?

I had the opportunity to enjoy a ceramics class hosted by the hotel where my family and I stayed on a recent vacation. It was a novel opportunity. Guests choose an unfinished piece of clay and paint it onsite. The staff then fires the raw items in a kiln overnight and they are ready to be picked up the next day. I'm not an artist by any stretch of the imagination, but I decided to give it a go. I selected an oversized coffee mug because, after all, who can't use another ugly mug at home? Using one of their samples as a guide, I carefully chose a stencil with an art deco font. I pictured a black mug with a cool saying on its front and polka dots of every color imaginable on its back. The walls of the classroom were covered with examples and photos of projects customers had created, proudly displayed as a "WOW" board. In my fantasy world, my finished mug would be so cool it would be exhibited as a sample for others to emulate.

Now the tough part: what words to stencil on it? *My name? That's too mundane. Famous quote? Not creative enough. My own quote? Stupid.* I sat back and thought for a minute. *There must be something unique I can put on this mug.*

Earlier in the week, I had shared a specific struggle I was facing with my friend, Merit. She encouraged me with a suggestion I found rather intriguing: Require More of Yourself. "What a fantastic inspirational phrase. That's what I will put on the side of my mug and I'll use it as a motivator when I am tempted to break promises to myself," I thought.

With a renewed sense of energy, I began my craft as if I were the next Picasso. "Careful with the stencil, strategic with the dots," I told myself as I created my beautiful piece and left it to face the kiln's heat.

The next morning I awoke eager to see the results of my labor. My little girl, Ellie, accompanied me to the classroom where an instructor removed it from the shelf and held it out for my inspection. It looked great to me. Ellie, being an advanced reader and more detail oriented than I am, quickly pointed out two letters I had transposed in error. She read out loud, "Require More of Yours_lef_"—that's right, a typo on my *hand-stenciled* mug. I was aghast. My masterpiece was ruined...and then, I realized the irony of my mistake. If I had required more of myself, I'd have been more careful, paid closer attention and not made the spelling error. The instructor was surprised by my disappointment because she thought I had misspelled on purpose. The funniest part of the whole story is that attached to my receipt was a note asking me to sign a permission slip allowing the instructor to take a picture of my project and display it on the "WOW" board. Evidently, someone thought the transposition was so clever that it would make a good sample. So I did make it to the "WOW" board after all, just not in the way I intended.

The best way I have found to require more of myself is to treat myself as I would treat a trusted friend. Accountability is the secret. I have had several accountability partners in my business life and they have been critical to my continued success. We meet once a month in person or by phone and share successes, challenges, and frustrations. Each of us has a specific length of time focused 100 percent on her or his agenda. Then we switch and repeat. We ask each other tough questions, give impressions, and suggestions; most importantly, we hold each other accountable to what was planned the month before. After years of different accountability partners, I have discovered a hidden gift. Each ally gives me grace. They give me permission to fail, a safe harbor where raw truth is accepted, and they provide the support I need to keep trying. Requiring more of myself is the same process, but without the help of a partner.

Are you generous enough to give yourself grace?

ask yourself...

In what ways might I require more of myself?

In what areas do I need to let current expectations rest?

What are the direct benefits I want to receive from each of the actions I've listed above?

Who would make a good accountability partner and do I want to try this idea?

"When you set an intention, when
you commit, the entire universe
conspires to make it happen."

~Sandy Forster
Australian Author &
Award-Winning Entrepreneur

Living with Personal Intention

Have you given much thought to the end of your life? I don't mean the fear of the unknown or the potential for pain. I am referring to the end of your life, the absence of the opportunity to act. Are you making choices today that reflect your legacy? One of my favorite television shows is *Inside the Actors Studio*, hosted by James Lipton. At the end of every episode, he presents the same set of questions to each celebrity guest. The final question on the quiz is very intriguing to me: "If Heaven exists, what do you hope God will say when you arrive at the Pearly Gates?"

Although many actors on the show answer in jest, I believe contemplating the answer for a period of time is likely to provide a more heartfelt response. I hadn't given much thought to my mortality until the summer of 1986 when I faced a near-death experience.

I had the opportunity to whitewater raft in Wisconsin with a group of friends. The beginning of the ride was smooth, even fun. I'm a good swimmer and have never been afraid to jump into lakes or pools. In the middle of our raft ride down the Menominee River, there is a legendary twelve-foot waterfall called Piers Gorge, a fancy name that should translate into *death wish ahead*. The gorge includes three drops in a row. They told us to anticipate a descent of twelve feet, seven feet, and five feet, in that order. That may not sound like much, but when all you have is one handle on the raft and an oar in the other hand, it's a bigger drop than you think.

At the top of the death fall, they beached the boats and gave us the option of walking down a trail if we were too nervous to raft. I wasn't nervous. I opted to give it a whirl. I yelled, "Ride on, baby!" and jumped into a boat with my boyfriend. Our first cruise down was the ultimate high in outdoor entertainment. As we glided over the initial fall I screamed, "Yee-haw!" like a cowgirl on her first bull. Surrounded by the deafening sound of crashing water, we arrived safely at the bottom of the three-tiered drop, disappointed it was over so fast. The guide said that because so many people had come down on foot, he was inviting us to run back up the huge hill and help bring the rest of the boats back down. He didn't have to ask us twice. We bolted back up to the summit. Several boats launched, and by the time we got to the front of the line, there was only one boat left. The problem was that the last boat was designed for only seven rafters and there were nine of us still at the top of the hill. The guide hesitated, which should have been my first warning. Then he decided that since we had all been down the falls once, we knew what to expect. He allowed all nine of us to crowd into the boat, a critical error in judgment. By bad luck of the draw, my man and I were the only ones without a strap to grasp onto or an oar to hold.

The guide flippantly said, "Just hang onto the person next to you and you'll be fine." That would have been true if the two girls in the front of the boat had kept their oars in the water like they were supposed to do. However, as soon as we reached the top of the first drop, they became scared and pulled up their paddles. By doing this, the nose of the raft lifted up at the wrong moment. (Friends watching from the shore told us the front three-quarters of the raft lifted completely out of the water.) I sat in the middle of the back bench, looking straight up, and instead of seeing sky, I saw the front bench of people falling backward. Since everyone had something to hold onto, they tossed around a bit but remained inside the vessel. Unfortunately, my date and I had nothing to grab but air. We both fell out of the raft into the calm, yet fast-moving water at the mouth of the falls. At first I laughed. Then reality hit and an alarm registered.

There was no chance of catching up to the boat. I watched the raft go over the falls accompanied by the hum of screaming passengers. Then all was quiet for a moment. In my mind I furiously reviewed the information covered during pre-launch training. The guide instructed us to follow these rules in the unlikely event of an overboard: (1) Breathe. *Check.* (2) Turn and put your back toward the flow of the water. *Check.* (3) Float on your back and rely on your life vest to work as a flotation device. *Check.* (4) Remain calm and wait for rescue. *Yeah, right.*

My friend was quickly dragged over an assortment of jagged rocks, gashing his back and arms. I fortunately remained in the middle of the river and rode smoothly until the first drop. If you think twelve feet doesn't sound like a lot, you should see what it looks like from the perspective of a fish! It feels like a gigantic waterslide at your favorite waterpark, only the water is not chlorine blue and there is no cute lifeguard at the bottom waiting to help you up when you stop. I have never quite pieced together what happened after my descent began. Those on the shore reported they could see my yellow helmet surface and disappear several times, and that I was moving really fast. From my perspective, the event unfolded in slow motion. I rode the first drop pretty well but got stuck in the eddies at the base. Eddies are small whirlpools of water that circulate very rapidly and make it difficult to move with the current. I kept fighting to get to the surface for air, but when my head reached the surface, the tow dragged me back down again and again. It was after my third try that I realized I was going to drown. My thoughts were: "No way, I can't drown. I can make it." I was all fight, fight, fight, but I needed air; I swam harder. The next seconds felt like minutes. While fighting the current, I focused only on me. I thought: "This is how I'm going to die." Next thought: "Who would have thought this would be the way I'd go?" As the water became tougher to fight, my mind shifted to others. "My family will be so sad. My death will affect the rest of their lives." Then the force of the eddies pushed me down so deep that my surroundings and mindset changed. It was ice cold, pitch black, and silent below the surface. I remember the silence the most. "How can it be silent? Is it really silent, or am I experiencing a lack of oxygen?" What followed these thoughts was the most wonderful feeling of peace. Complete bliss. No worries, no fear, no pain, nothing but deep satisfaction. I never saw a tunnel of light. My life didn't flash before my eyes. How close I was to leaving earth, I'll never know.

This entire saga transpired in only a few short minutes but it was packed with a full cycle of emotion: fear, fight, astonishment, peace—in that order. I have a friend who once choked on a piece of meat and almost died in a restaurant bathroom. When recounting her story, she expressed the same exact emotions I experienced. Interestingly, what we both remember most about our near-death experience was the sense of peace we felt.

My peace was quickly shattered when my body finally caught up to the boat and I smacked into its side without warning. It turns out that the rafters held their position the best they could in the calm waters at the bottom of the third fall. I heard someone yelling, "Get her in the boat! Get her in the boat!" The voice, a faraway echo, was a fellow rafter. Urgently, several people grabbed my life jacket, and pulled me onboard. I struggled for air and eventually water spurted out with a cough. I was shaken at first, but quickly calmed down in time to help rescue my friend as well. Although he was slightly bloody, he was fine too. My near-death experience has left me with two things: one, no desire to ever raft again; and two, a sense of calm regarding death. When my time comes, I hope it turns out to be as peaceful, and might I say, wonderful.

I have given a lot of thought to how I would answer the final question if I were to appear on *Inside the Actors Studio*: "If Heaven exists, what I do hope to hear God say when I arrive at the Pearly Gates?"

I'd answer: "Your Mom's waiting for you on the first tee and boy does she have a story for you."

When a friend heard my perilous story, she said the right question to ask at the end of this chapter should be: Are you living with personal intention? Remove the humor with which the actors answered James Lipton's final question on *Inside the Actors Studio* and seriously focus on the legacy of your life and you may find a different answer.

Are you currently living a life that serves the sentence
you hope to hear God say when you arrive at the Pearly Gates?

—————————————————————— ask yourself...

If Heaven exists, what do I hope God will say when I arrive at the
Pearly Gates?

Am I living with the intention I most want to achieve?

When I focus on the legacy of my life, what do I want it to be?

What needs to change for me to live my desired intention?

Exercise

no.4

Pyramid to Ponder

Build a pyramid of thoughts about yourself. Start with a ten-word phrase. The next line down can only have nine words in the sentence. Keep decreasing by one word until you reach the bottom.

NO ONE CAN STOP ME FROM BEING A BETTER PERSON

I CAN MASTER THE FINE ART OF REALLY LIVING

FIVE SHORT WORDS, I GET WHAT I TOLERATE

WISHING, NOT THE SAME AS TAKING ACTION

TODAY IS THE DAY OF RECKONING

IT IS ALWAYS ABOUT INTENTION

SOMETIMES LIFE'S NOT FAIR

SEE THE POSSIBILITIES

MAINTAIN FOCUS

RELEASE

Exercise

no.5

Creating a Physical Refurbishment Plan

Does a fresh start mean an external makeover in addition to an internal restart? I tried this exercise at one of my ocean retreats and found it to be quite helpful in giving my outer self permission to refresh itself at the same time I was working on my inner self.

Start at the very top of your head and slowly work your way mentally down your body, stopping at every part to evaluate. You can do this with your eyes closed in meditation position or you can actually use a mirror and view yourself with a fresh perspective. Make a list of all the things you need to do to bring your outer self toward the appearance you desire. This list does not commit you to take action. This list is simply part of an exercise that forces you to take a closer look at needs that might be holding you back from a complete reset.

It's important that when you are done with this repair list, you also ask "What *is good* about my outer self?" Otherwise, this exercise can be depressing. You may say to yourself, "Where can I trade this model in for a new one?" Guess what? There's no trade-in, just refurbishment. So call it your refurbishing plan and begin to pluck away at your list. Why wait until next month or next year?

Exercise

no.6

Write a Letter to Yourself

While the act of writing a letter to yourself has been around for a long time, I haven't heard many people say they've actually done it. I, too, had never written a letter to myself until it was time to write about this exercise for the book. It would seem unfair to suggest you do something I have not done myself.

Write your letter from the future you to the present day you. There are many examples of this exercise online, but my suggestion is that you *do not* research it first. Write it your own way, in your own words. Remember there is no right or wrong. The object of the letter is to talk to yourself the way you would talk to an old friend. You should use words that are supportive and complimentary, not negative and deprecating. Pretend you are nearing the end of your life and reflect backward.

To help you get started I have provided an example opening, but I purposely did not give you the whole letter in order to avoid influencing your own style. Finally, I suggest you write this down using ink and stationery instead of typing it into a document. Years later, seeing your own mark will carry a greater significance. See the example on the next page.

Hello Old Friend,

How have the years passed so fast for us? It seems like just yesterday we were making all kinds of mental plans for things we would do someday, when we had time. I am so proud of you for chasing your dreams and not sitting around just wishing. You have been so good at keeping your commitments to others. Faithfulness, loyalty, supportiveness, and creativity have been of great value to those who love you. I know there are some areas of your life that you are beating yourself up about and that you wish different choices had been made. Put that behind you now and focus on the gift your life has been. If I were to write your life's story for others to read I would include a chapter on your successes including: (Make your bullet list here and then continue your letter to yourself.)

Job well done,
Your Future Self

_____ my letter...

Planning Your Life &
Finding Focus

"Every thought is a seed.
If you plant crab apples,
don't count on harvesting
Golden Delicious."

~Billy Meyer
American Baseball
Player & Coach
1893–1957

Creating a Life Filled with Hope

Do you agree that many of us spend a large portion of our time living in the ordinary zone? Work, chores, personal care, and mundane conversations with others are all part of an ordinary day. It is when we allow our days to bleed together and become a never-ending sequence of same old, same old that negative symptoms, boredom, fatigue, irritability, and even depression and hopelessness, seep into our lives.

However, even though most of life takes place in the ordinary zone, *we can create fertile ground for the extraordinary simply by deliberate behavior.* "What does my life in the extraordinary zone look and feel like?" I thought about this question on a Sunday morning during church. My thoughts drifted from the sermon and I was pondering the concept of a contented life when I noticed the children of the congregation lining up at the front. The song they sang instantly took me back to my youth. I hadn't heard this old favorite in years; "This little light of mine, I'm gonna let it shine…" The word *shine* resounded and that's when it hit me. When I'm in my extraordinary zone, I *shine*.

What does *shine* mean to me? I asked myself. Instantly words come to mind. I jotted them down on the back of the bulletin without processing at all; peace, focus, hope, energy, free of big struggle.

On a bright morning several weeks later, as I watched the sunrise, I contemplated my spontaneous personal definition of the words I had written.

Peace
—free of the internal struggle of indecision and confusion;
not knowing the next step

I closed my eyes, inhaled deeply, exhaled slowly, dropped my shoulders, and rolled my head forward. I felt a sense of release and surrender. I asked myself: "What intentional behavior is needed to gain peace in my life?"

I decided to focus on my areas of indecision and confusion. Analyzing the causes and solutions for each of these and, most importantly, making a decision about the next step quickly brought me peace.

Focus
—having a detailed 1-2-3 plan and being able
to carry out the strategy one action at a time

A cookbook, step-by-step approach makes me happy. "What intentional behavior is needed to gain focus in my life?" I asked myself.

Setting my priorities, then creating a list of chronological steps, just like a recipe, is a simple answer. Please note: I said simple, not easy; there is a difference. It took quite a while to identify all the steps in my "focus formula" but once it was done, the process was clear.

Hope
—that things can get better, will get better, with the light of a new day.

"What intentional behavior is needed to bring hope back into my life?" I asked and then answered: "Believing in yourself and others is a big part of hope."

A dear friend was fighting cancer and the most important advice her oncologist gave her was, "Believe with every ounce of your being that you will win. Surround yourself with people who believe you will win." I loved his advice and integrated this lesson into my own life. I began to spend less time with people who are negative and hopeless.

Energy
—being able to dig deep to find the power to keep moving forward

Tired is what many people described as their current status when I was doing research for this book. They told me they were physically, mentally, emotionally, and spiritually tired.

How to get through *it* when one is depleted is the challenge. Is it possible that it is just about taking care of yourself? I asked my friend Ken Carlson, a certified life coach, to tell me more about the concept of "giving myself permission." This was his response:

> Realizing that the answer to lowering anxiety isn't found "out there". It isn't found by making one more person happy. It isn't found by rescuing one more person in need. The first step is saying to yourself, "I am the problem"…and then with a hopeful tone…"I am the solution."

> Giving yourself permission is about giving yourself the care, concern, time, and energy you wouldn't hesitate to give to others that you love. Giving yourself permission may seem selfish—but in the end it is a gift to others far beyond what you are giving them today. An empty pitcher can't fill up anything, but a full pitcher can refresh multiple cups.

> So what does it look like to give yourself permission? It is a little bit different for each person, but here are a few ideas:

Will you give yourself permission to take just one day a week for yourself to recharge, to fully play?

Will you give yourself permission to sleep in, or take an afternoon nap, or to form the habit of going to bed at 8 o'clock? Sleep is soul-care. Often we feel like we are wasting precious time when we sleep. Nonsense—we are rebuilding ourselves.

Will you give yourself permission to practice silence and solitude regularly? This gift to your soul has no downside. When we learn that we are okay even when we aren't making others happy or sharing our knowledge with them—we learn so much about our own place in our world.

Will you give yourself permission to say "Yes"—over and over again—to things that you love that you have been denying yourself?

Will you give yourself permission to say "No" to people and situations you actually don't like? Can you find the courage to stand up for yourself and be honest?

I'm excited to see my clients change as they give themselves permission to be their true selves—to connect with their own wiring. I encourage you to give it a shot!

As a final note, I'd like to share an experience I had a few years ago while working in corporate America. I received a motivational poem in my email. The poem said all the right things to get me off my butt—along the lines of "the early bird gets the worm"—and inspire me to work hard. But the message most of us really need to hear is a message of slowing down—a message of self-care. So I took the poem and changed it, and sent it out—much to the chagrin of my department heads. I will end with the poem I wrote.

Rest
while others are striving

Sleep
while others are competing

Relax
while others are stressing

Love
while others are fighting

Let go
while others are holding tight

Dream
while others are marching in step

Hope
while others are scheming

See beauty
while others see nothing

Be
while others do

Live joyfully
while others barely live

Thank you, Ken, for sharing the great insight and wonderful poem. In order to achieve 80 percent in the *extraordinary zone,* we need to create fertile ground. This is done by creating a plan of *intentional behavior.*

Giving others hope is the main reason I felt called to write this book. It was almost ten years in the making and at different times I would share portions of the half-baked manuscript with special people in my life. I even planned several retreats for friends who were struggling, so I could see if the content within the book was of value to them. This passage is shared with permission from a friend who experienced one of my retreats:

I was in desperate need of healing, rejuvenating, and getting some of my energy back. My mother had just passed away and the past couple months of stress had definitely taken a major toll on my health and well-being. Laurie offered to plan a retreat for me and I decided that I absolutely had to get away and restore my energy. The book contained so many inspiring ideas and it calmed me just to read about all the nurturing things I could do for myself. I picked out three chapters to read and exercises I wanted to put my own spin on. She reserved a night at a quaint historic hotel on a beautiful river. When I arrived, she had set up a plate of cheeses, fruit, chocolates, and a bottle of wine on the balcony and had a gift bag on the table. Inside, each gift was marked to indicate when I should open it. The first gift bag contained an envelope which said, "Relax, have some wine and cheese and go to the spa at 7:00 for a fabulous massage!" I was thrilled. I sat on the balcony and read from Laurie's book before my massage. I was already entering a zone, just putting aside time for myself, and cherishing the guidance from the book. There was also a personal journal, coasters made from the flowers from my mom's funeral, and a coffee mug, which said "Relaunching Now!" inside the gift bag. All of these personal gifts brought tears to my eyes.

After the massage, I wrote down my goals and dreams and put them in the special box I had brought. I did Laurie's happiness exercise, and I wrote down my idea of peace and happiness on beautiful stationery and put them in the box. I sat by the fire and imagined all of the fear, worry, stress, sadness, anger, and exhaustion going up in smoke.

In the morning I took a Jacuzzi and imagined the jets sending white positive energy through the bottoms of my feet and circulating through my whole body. I let my whole body fill with wonderful energy. When I pulled the plug in the bathtub, I imagined all exhaustion and negative energy going right down the drain. Then I took a shower and had the pure clean water cleanse me from head to toe, rejuvenating and launching me into a future of positive energy. I felt my mom was at peace and it was now my time to find peace.

Once you have determined the surrounding that fits your needs, you can begin the process of reviving hope. Do what it takes to spend a day, or a longer period of time, in the setting that gives you the best chance for rejuvenation and hope. Start by answering these questions, being as specific as you can.

Creating a life filled with hope starts with assembling an environment where peace can find its way to you.

——————————————————————— a s k   y o u r s e l f . . .

What does *shine* mean to me?

What in my life helps me shine?

What additional peace do I want in my life?

What intentional changes will give me greater peace?

What intentional behavior will help me focus my precious time and energy even more?

What intentional behavior will give greater hope to my life?

_____ thoughts...

"It takes so much energy
to be what you are not.
It takes so little to be
what you truly are."

~Dr. Phil McGraw
Psychologist & Author

Who Do You Aspire to Be?

"Finish what you start" has always been our family's policy. Sports, clubs and classes must be seen through to the end.

When our son Evan was eleven, he started playing the trombone. The band teacher was warm-hearted, and taught passionately. Evan was eager to play, and like many children, he promised to practice faithfully. The following year, the band teacher was promoted to high school level and a first year teacher arrived. Within a short time, Evan expressed resentment, lack of interest, and had limited motivation. After a misunderstanding mid-year and a condescending email from the teacher to us, we sat down with Evan to discuss his challenges.

With great parental wisdom, Tom said, "Without practice you are not going to be very good." My son mulled that over for a minute, and with great maturity he said "I don't want to be one of the greats, Dad, I just want to be an average Joe." Tom frowned. I laughed out loud. It struck me as funny because so many people go through life picturing themselves as a success. They play sports in the backyard, recreating a scene where they score the touchdown in the final seconds or hit the grand-slam homerun in the bottom of the ninth inning. I've acted out the fifty-foot putt I would sink to win the LPGA golf tournament against Nancy Lopez many times. Now, here is my boy saying, "I like average." His dad saw it as a comment born from laziness; I interpreted it as blunt honesty.

Now is the time for your blunt honesty. Do you aspire to be an Alexander the Great or an Average Joe? Do you truly desire to be great at something?

When I say great, I don't mean you have to be best in the world, famous like a pro athlete, or an award-winning actress. I simply mean, do you want to do what it takes to be your very best? Yes or no? It is important to realize that either answer is fine as long as you are honest with yourself.

It is okay to accept average. I'm sure it surprises you to hear a motivational speaker utter such blasphemy. But I honestly believe the upside of Evan's "Average Joe mindset" is that he is content with himself. He is happy, not competitive, like many his age. He is comfortable in his own skin instead of defeated by unmet goals. It isn't that he doesn't have goals. He is an honor student and an Eagle Scout with good values and a kind heart. Why can't that be enough? It can be, if *you* so choose. I'm making an assumption that most readers of this book are adults. Here is one major advantage of being an adult—you get to make your own choices. By the same token, you'll face any consequences that come from the decisions you make. Many people I talk to about a decision they're contemplating put heavy emphasis on other people's opinions. Parents' opinions rate high on the influence list. The balance between pushing to succeed and supporting people as they are can be tricky. If you know in your heart that an action you're contemplating is only a wish and you are unwilling to put in the work to achieve it, call yourself "Joe" and move on. I know many wonderful, happy, and content Joes.

On the flip side, when you have a goal or a dream and you are willing to do what it takes to accomplish it, nothing can stop you. Country singer Tim McGraw recorded a song that motivates me when I am twenty-two minutes into the elliptical workout and swear I cannot move my butt for one more minute. The song is titled, "How Bad Do You Want It?" The chorus asks: "How bad do you want it? How bad do you need it? Are you sleeping, eating, dreaming with that one thing on your mind?" Ah, the secret formula to greatness revealed in the lyrics of a country song.

According to *Forbes* magazine, almost two-thirds of the world's billionaires made their fortunes from scratch, relying on grit and determination. I'm motivated by stories of determination that have nothing to do with money or fame. "Dream big" is an age-old adage. Who hasn't heard a speaker spout a "be all you can be" phrase? Hasn't everyone picked up a book in the self-help section at one time or another that tells you how to obtain your goals? Of all the things I have ever read on this topic, there is one solid exercise that I do on a regular basis to work toward any lofty goal. I call it *back-it-in dreaming*. Let me show you how to back-it-in dream by using an abbreviated version of my own example.

WRITE DOWN YOUR ULTIMATE GOAL OR DREAM.

My goal and dream is to own a retreat center on the ocean. I visualize a waiting list to get in and people coming from all over the country to stay at my theme-focused getaway. It is well known throughout the country, and it is profitable enough that I work when I want to and have time off when I need it.

KNOCK THIS DREAM DOWN ONE STEP.

I don't own the center; I rent a facility owned by someone else in unique locations. Rest of dream is same as written in #1.

REDUCE THE VISION BY ONE MORE STEP

I'll rent a retreat site that is close to my home and host one event there within the next year. I will have to find my own audience and determine a fee that will meet expenses yet be affordable to attendees.

KEEP REDUCING BY ONE SMALL STEP UNTIL YOU GET TO A LEVEL THAT IS POSSIBLE IN THE NEAR FUTURE.

Offer a retreat session to an appropriate client who already has a group looking for a retreat. Once you get it boiled down to something easily obtained, write down your next executable step. In other words, what can you do <u>now</u>?

The back-it-in exercise I have described may sound easy, but when you actually sit down to dream it, and write it down, it is amazing how many mental blocks one can encounter. My advice is to break through the block by being brave. Don't hesitate to think big and remember you are not required to share the ideas with anyone if you don't want to. Self-consciousness is what I believe causes people to stop short in pursuing their dreams. Just ask yourself these questions to get motivated to act.

How bad do you want it?

_____ a s k   y o u r s e l f . . .

Specifically, what do I want to accomplish?

On a scale of 1–10 (10 is high), what is my desire to accomplish this goal?

What blessings/gifts/rewards will I receive from the accomplishment of this goal?

What sacrifice and/or effort does this goal require?

What does my "back-it-in dream" look like on paper?

"The truth of what
one says lies in
what one does."

~Bernhard Schlink
German Author (b. 1944) in
Der Vorleser (tr. The Reader)

Define Yourself

One day, while watching a television interview, I heard someone say, "I am going to take back what defines me." I no longer remember the show or what the interview was about, but I am intrigued by the concept of defining oneself. We regularly consult dictionaries to look up the timeless definitions of words and rely on their accuracy and consistency. By contrast, our personal definition changes throughout the stages of our lives. I created a short list to define myself at each major milestone of my life, from birth to present day. When completed, I reviewed the list and experienced a wash of positive emotion.

I noticed all of my defining titles were roles I filled: friend, wife, mother, coworker—not definitions of *who I really am*. How do I define myself today? After several weeks of mulling this over, I still wasn't coming up with a decent response, so I decided to take the question to the streets. I asked this question of many people: "If I were to look up (insert their name) in the dictionary, what would it say?" I heard lots of great answers, but my favorite came from a wonderful woman named Sharon Carter, a friend and professional speaker from Arkansas. When I asked her the question, she gave it ten seconds of thoughtful reflection and then, with her beautiful southern twang, she said,

"Sharon Carter is a builder of people."

What a great statement. I had defined myself by a list of roles rather than the value of my actions, but she had defined herself using a fantastic personal attribute—*builder of people*. It turned my thinking upside down and challenged me to process the question again from a different viewpoint. I believe that if a dictionary of this kind of definition existed and you looked up my name, it would say, "Laurie Guest is an experiencer of life." (I know experiencer isn't even a real word, but it should be.) I have had lots of interesting experiences because I maintain a "life list."

Most everyone has heard the term "bucket list," made popular by a 1997 movie directed by Rob Reiner about two old men who create a list of things to do before they die. It's a catchy phrase and it is a list I believe everyone should make. Have you? Sure, there are things you would like to do someday, but have you taken the time to complete a written life list? Actively working my life list has been one of the great joys of my existence. How many of us are guilty of saying things like, "That's something I have always wanted to do." Or, "I'd like to do such-and-such someday." But what if someday never comes?

Years ago, a neighbor of mine who had three small girls fought a five-year battle against cancer. I was told by those closest to her that once she knew the diagnosis was terminal, she began writing letters to each of her girls designed to be opened on the milestone days of their lives, the big days that she wouldn't witness. First dates, graduations, wedding days, and the birth of their children are the types of events I imagine she included. I was so moved by her generosity of spirit and the strength it must have taken for her to complete this task that when I saw Cathy for the last time I could not express myself adequately. I would have liked to tell Cathy that her behavior influenced my conduct in regards to my own life, that is, it caused me to take charge of making things happen instead of waiting for *someday* when these things would be more affordable, easier, or less subject to the pressure of competing obligations. Cathy was forty-two years old when she passed away, and she is often in the back of my mind reminding me to love better and live better.

It was shortly after her passing that I wrote down some of the things I wanted to do "someday," and I got to the work of making them happen. Some of the things on my life list are 100 percent in my control and can be accomplished with relative ease. Trips to Yellowstone, taking a photography class, and learning to play piano are just a few examples. The next level of activities includes things that are doable, but they will take a little more time to complete. For example, publish a book and invent a game that sells in the marketplace. And then there is the top tier of my life list. These are the dream ideas, the ones that are mostly out of my control and unlikely to happen. One such example was my desire to see a live taping of the *Oprah Winfrey Show*. Since I live only about an hour outside of Chicago, I was eligible to have my name on a standby list for last minute audience calls. Years came and went and there wasn't ever a request for my butt in the seat at Oprah.

My niece Lauren is one of the people I love most in the world, and she also maintains a life list. Seeing the *Oprah Winfrey Show* live is one of the items that appeared on both of our lists. When we heard that 2011 would be the last year the show would air, we knew the odds of getting tickets were slim. Instead of being discouraged, we compromised by attending her "Live Your Best Life Weekend" in New York City. This was an event connected to her magazine rather than the show. As luck would have it, we ended up in the front row and saw her in person no more than twenty yards away. That had to count as good enough for the life list and I crossed it off, but I felt like a cheat because it wasn't the same as seeing the show.

In May of 2011, Oprah was winding up her long TV run with quite a bit of fanfare. There were special guests on the show all year long and a star-studded tribute to her at the United Center. We tried to get tickets, but failed. Then, four days before the final taping, Lauren called to tell me she had scored Oprah tickets for the final show. I assumed she was a victim of a hoax and did not join in her enthusiasm. The odds of getting a ticket to this once-in-a-lifetime event were like winning the lottery. After trying on a regular basis for a quarter of a century, I found it impossible to believe the hottest tickets in the country landed in her hands. I agreed to accompany her to the studio on the specific date but warned her not to be too disappointed if, when we got there, the doors to the studio were locked. I was sure the final taping had been done the week before and didn't believe this was an actual opportunity.

We left early that morning and arrived at the studio to find a line of people waiting for standby tickets. I started to think this might be real. We waited. We wondered. We hoped.

More people with tickets began to arrive and with them came an anticipation that was palpable. Of all the life list activities I have completed, I must say this one had the most excitement brewing around it. The slim chance of us achieving this goal, coupled with the fact the final taping was a television milestone, created a once-in-a-lifetime opportunity.

Before I knew it the studio doors opened and we were invited in to witness history. Whether you are an Oprah fan or not, one cannot deny the awe of a poor girl from Mississippi navigating a career of influence the way O has done. To watch her skillfully monologue an hour-long program from the heart was like watching a famous artist paint a canvas. It made me feel *fortunate* to be there. To listen to her craft words into sentences that spoke to each of us differently was like listening to a musician play a concerto, and it made me feel *peaceful*. But most of all, I experienced an "in the moment" feeling like none I have ever felt before.

We were not allowed to have cell phones or cameras in the studio, so instead of trying to peek through a camera lens, I truly experienced the moment and logged it into memory, which is powerful. No one in the audience considered talking during the taping or moving about. There were no distractions. The energy in the room was focused and on high octane. The studio only holds about 350 people, so the setting was intimate and every person felt privileged to be there.

We would have experienced none of this if Lauren and I hadn't been working our life lists. Have you given any thought to what you would like to include on your life list? Each of our lists are unique to us but what we have in common is the fun of creating the list and working it. The things on my bucket list are *how* I experience and enjoy life. If I chose not to work my list, I'm afraid one day would blend in to the next until the opportunities had passed me by. So, I define myself as an experiencer of life.

"Gratitude is the single greatest treasure I will take with me from this experience."

Oprah Winfrey
From her final show, May 25, 2011

_____ a s k   y o u r s e l f . . .

If I discovered my name in the dictionary, how would I be defined, as of today?

What do I want the definition to be?

What do I want on my life list, my "bucket list"?

How will I turn wishes into action for the experiences I most want?

———————————————— thoughts...

"Nothing ever becomes real
'til it is experienced."

~John Keats
English Poet
1795–1821

My Must-Act Guide

Why isn't there a word in the English language that means *one small step at a time*? Sure, we have well-known phrases that mean the same thing. Baby steps, bite-size pieces, and an inch at a time are all great examples. The concept of *one small step at a time* is basic, but its value is often overlooked because of its simplicity.

Once, when I was overwhelmed with indecision and confusion in a particular area of my life, a friend suggested I list all of the actions I needed to take to bring order to the chaos. Then he advised me to take the list and start crossing off my entries one at a time until clarity came. Even as I write this, I am rolling my eyes much the same way I expressed myself to him at the time.

How is this different from a to-do list, a pro versus con exercise, or a Sunburst Sort-Out grid like the one I shared in an earlier chapter? It's different from a to-do list in that it stands alone. The actions are not mixed up with chores and errands like grocery shopping and dental appointments. It's grander than a to-do list. It is a "must-act guide."

It's different from a pro versus con exercise because it isn't a tool to settle indecision. Any debate is over long before the action list is created. For example, one of the issues I was dealing with was my health. A borderline blood test, a family history of diabetes and high blood pressure, the delay of my annual check-up, and a host of other issues weighed heavily on my mind. There was *no debate* about whether I should get my act together; it was a question of *how*. Putting my action list in a logical order of actions was the first step toward resolution.

It's different from the Sunburst Sort-Out diagram because I wasn't being pulled away from the action by anyone other than myself. Once I had my list, it became all about the bite-size pieces. Looking at only one item and taking action to complete it made the mountain of issues easier to handle. I suppose this is similar to the answer to the proverbial question, "How does one eat an elephant? One bite at a time." Once my first entry was taken care of, I simply moved on to the next until the list was completed.

Every accomplishment begins with an action.

_____ ask yourself...

What overwhelming project or issue lies before me?

What are the bite-size actions I need to take to resolve this daunting task?

What is the logical order of the steps I need to take?

"If you haven't time
to respond to a tug at
your pants leg, your
schedule is too crowded."

~Robert Brault
American Writer

Looking for the Hidden Message

For as long as I can remember, I have looked for the hidden messages in life. I'm quite certain I could fill an entire book with amazing anecdotes of symbolic messages. The key is to open your eyes, ears, and heart to receive and be enlightened by the lessons. Taking the time to journal what I have seen and the message I absorbed at the time usually brings a flash of insight. Here is a passage from a three-day retreat I took in California in 2003. I'm sharing it almost exactly as it reads in my journal:

> I had high hopes of being able to perform a silent poolside meditation both of the afternoons I was here. When it didn't work out yesterday, I was frustrated. There were women all around the pool talking on cell phones, chatting, and laughing with each other. I was so distracted I couldn't even begin to do the retreat exercises I had planned. Even though I moved my chair <u>twice</u> in an effort to drown them out, it didn't work!
>
> Today I headed to the other of the two pools. I found a really loud screaming kid, and no matter how hard I tried to tune him out, I couldn't. "What do I need right now?" I ask myself. I need peace. I need quiet. I am frustrated that I can't find it. I think this is what sums up my life right now—I need time to assess what I need and want.
>
> In the middle of writing the last paragraph, the loud child left. It is silent except for some traffic nearby and the rustle of leaves and newspapers blowing on the concrete behind me. Time to try focusing again. It is much harder than I thought to relax and turn my brain off.

Amazing—as soon as I'm starting to get into the groove, the child returns to the pool. Quiet this time, his mother is encouraging him to nap. Is it possible, for the second day in a row, that the message I am to receive is coming in the form of this child's action and I am pushing it away? I still feel irritation that this whole area is not all mine. Why? There is plenty of space and really no noise my headphones can't compensate for. What's the real issue? Do I not want to share the space? I feel I am searching for peace. Almost frantic to find it. What do I need in my life right now? While I am deep in thought, the child approaches and gets in the pool right next to my chaise. Instead of seeing him as a distraction, I am trying to see him as a messenger. I decide that whatever he says or does will be the message I am supposed to hear today. The suspense builds—how profound will it be? He smiles at me and looks down. Then he glances back up and in the most innocent voice asks, "Isn't Mr. Incredible fat?" (Mr. Incredible being the main character of the new Disney film at the time—and yes, he is huge.) "In the commercial he pulls his belt like this!" he says, as he tugs his trunks out in front of him as far as they will go. "UGGH!" he adds. Then the messenger boy snaps his trunks shut and swims away.

Yeah, that's a message all right. I'm smiling at the ironic nature of the communication. My distractions are my problem. Conquer them, and I can have everything I wrote down on my life list. None of it is impossible, and achieving it would be incredible, for sure.

Day three on my retreat and I am eager to see what message I will find today, now that I am open to soaking up the environment around me instead of being irritated by those sharing my space.

I am lying in the sun meditating and concentrating on hearing or seeing today's intended message. I feel the breeze; it almost tickles. I open my eyes and see sun glistening through a palm tree. I hear the soft music in my headphones instead of the constant pool chatter. I close my eyes and connect with my environment. Suddenly, I turn my head for no reason and spot a small girl poolside. Jean shorts, green shirt with a huge 77 printed on the front, splashing her feet in the pool. The wind blows her long hair and she looks to the sky and then closes her eyes to the harsh glare. The sun is bright on her cheeks. She smiles to herself and splashes again. She looks like she is singing; although, I can't hear her. She seems so calm, so content. Content—good word. I feel tears come to my eyes, as I am homesick for my children after only a few days away. The little girl jumps up and begins to explore, walking the wall that surrounds the area. Her grandmother calls her over, whispers something, strokes her hair, and off she goes again, happy. I've taken my headphones off, straining to hear what she is saying, but I can't make it out. She is playing an imaginary game of some kind and loving it. She begins to come my way and I am excited to see what she will say to me, if anything. As she approaches, I am almost giddy inside with anticipation of the cool hidden meaning I will find in her words. First words I can hear her say are, "Two coins, and now we need a long dress." She is content, happy with herself in this moment. Slowly I drift off to sleep, uncertain if there is a message in her sentence. Sometime later, I wake to see the young girl and her grandma lying side by side on chaises. Grandma is totally still, resting. "77" is flopping all over, unable to lie still—too much energy, no time to waste. More than sixty years separates these two. A girl with so much to say, she can't stop, and an old woman who has said it all.

I turn my head to watch them a little longer, but they are gone. How could they disappear so quickly? No one left at the pool but me. I don't feel lonely; I feel alive.

We live in a culture that always pushes us to do rather than just be. I encourage you to take a break and just be. With a quiet mind, relax and look for the hidden messages that surround you. They are there if you will invite them into your reach. When you see, hear, or feel symbolic wisdom, write it down without processing it.

Allow yourself to just be
and see what insightful messages come to you.

_____ a s k y o u r s e l f...

What message did I hear when giving myself time to listen?

Is there an action I should take as a result of receiving this symbolic

wisdom?

Exercise

no.7

What Would Create the Best Life for Me?

Take no one else into consideration and don't be afraid to dream big.

When experiencing your best life:

Where do you live?

What do you do with your days?

How do you spend your nights?

Who is with you? Do you already know these people or do you need to meet them?

What does your home look like?

What do you look like?

Is there a skill you are learning?

What is important to you in this life you've created?

What are you proud of when you talk about yourself?

What did you give up to achieve this life?

What is stopping you from creating this life today?

Exercise

_____ no.8 _____

Creating a Vision Board

A vision board is a tool used to help you clarify, concentrate on, and maintain focus on a specific life goal. Literally, a vision board is any sort of board on which you display images that represent whatever you want to be, do, or have in your life.

What is the point of creating a vision board? Simply put, we tend to be very busy and are constantly bombarded by distractions. No matter how good our intentions, our reality is that, far too often, we live by default. We spend every day, all day, reacting to the immediate circumstances. Meanwhile, our hopes and dreams get lost in the shuffle, or forgotten altogether. Making use of vision boards serves several purposes, some of which include helping you to identify your vision and give it clarity, reinforcing your daily affirmations, and keeping your attention on your intentions.

VISION BOARDS HELP PROVIDE CLARITY

For example, saying "I want a better life" is a fine goal, but have you given serious thought to exactly what that means? Try to conjure up a mental image of what your "better life" looks like. Where are you? What do you see around you? What is taking place? Who is with you? How do you feel?

For some of us, it is surprisingly difficult to find such clarity. Making a vision board can be a tremendous help. In order to create my vision board, I must actively seek images that represent details of the new and improved life I foresee. That means narrowing it down to specifics. For some, a better life might mean having a new car or home. Others may be seeking a new relationship or improvements in existing relationships. Doubtless you have heard it said that most of us never get what we want because we don't know what we want. Making a vision board is a wonderful way to bring clarity to a general desire and transform that vague notion of "something better" into a clear vision of what you really want.

USE A VISION BOARD FOR YOUR DAILY AFFIRMATIONS

Once you dream it, the next step is to believe it. In addition to images, vision boards can include words, phrases or sentences that affirm your intentions. These "affirmations" are extremely important because the words we use in both speech and thought are very powerful. Unfortunately, more often than not, all the words in our heads are negative.

Somehow, we must silence the mind chatter that plagues us every minute of every waking hour. You know that little voice in your head that never shuts up, the one that supports and promotes all your limiting beliefs by repeating an endless litany of every shortcoming you could possibly have (and many that you couldn't possibly have) and every reason why you can't or shouldn't or won't ever be, do, or have what you really want.

Affirmations are the worst enemies of that little voice. By focusing on the positive, affirmations help turn your attention from the self-defeating to the self-empowering. Affirmations express who you really are, release you from those limiting beliefs, and allow you to know that the possibilities really are *unlimited*.

A VISION BOARD KEEPS YOU FOCUSED

Another key purpose that vision boards serve is to help you stay focused. It isn't difficult to start each day with a positive attitude—until you get out of bed. How quickly that fresh *new me* attitude can sink back into oblivion beneath the tasks and challenges of everyday life. How can you possibly remain focused on any goal while people and circumstances constantly pull you in dozens of directions at once? By using a vision board, of course!

No matter what happens during your day, you have a constant reminder of where you intend to be. Appealing to you on both conscious and subconscious levels, a vision board can work wonders toward keeping your mind focused on your goal, your attention on your intentions, and your life headed in the direction *you* choose.

What is a vision board?
It might just be the most important thing
you do for yourself this year!

Wishing you peace, joy, and abundance
in every aspect of your life!
~Susan LaBorde

For more information on how to make and use vision boards
to create a better life for yourself, visit Susan on the web at
www.MakeaVisionBoard.com.

Exercise

_____ no.9 _____

Personal Code of Ethics

Have you ever written down your personal code of ethics and read it out loud? I don't mean the Ten Commandments or your batting average. I mean the rules by which you live, no matter what. Living your word is powerful.

On the left side of your paper, write down as fast as you can all the things you believe to be true about you and your belief system. When you have completed your list, return to the top and make a second column titled "truth." Now dig deeper and write down the real truth about each of your beliefs. Here is an example:

BELIEF

I tell it like it is.

I do not steal.

Universe has a way of balancing things.

Keep commitments.

TRUTH

Sometimes I embellish for laughs as needed.

Item not put on bill, lucky me!

Some things in life don't make sense.

Make excuses.

When your list is complete, you will have a personal code of ethics. Where the flash of insight comes into play is when you have a rock-solid belief that doesn't match your behavior. It is common for us to feel strongly about something, yet we sometimes get off track in our actions. This exercise may help you put a spotlight on a need for a conduct modification.

_____ my personal code of ethics...

Rejuvenation &
Celebration

"At birth we are given
the awesome
privilege of enjoying
this world. What will you
do with your time?

~Debbie Ford
Author
1955-2013

How Can I Rejuvenate Myself? The Thrill of Theme Living

Several years ago, I started a tradition that I call "theme living." At the kickoff of a new year, I choose a personal theme to live by for the next 365 days. It isn't a resolution. Theme living is a concept that you *want* to adhere to that requires a change in thought, words, and deeds. My first year of theme living was "The Year of NO!" Every request made of me was processed through a time-commitment budget. Similar to a financial budget, the trick was not to give all the time away but to spend it purposefully. I determined the three priorities for my time: raising my two children, managing my business, and taking control of my health. If the request for my time did not fall into one of these three priorities, I said, "No."

"Can you bake three dozen cookies for the bake sale?"

"No, but I can stop by the bakery and get the fancy decorated cookies."

I've noticed that when I bring these cookies, they are often the first chosen by the children. I can also guarantee this store-bought treat is way better than anything I'll make from scratch. When I teach this idea at seminars, I always ask the crowd if they have trouble saying no. The question is always met with vigorous head bobbing.

So here is my script for saying no to requests for my time when I am unable or unwilling to say yes: "I'm sorry, I have to pass at this time, but please don't hesitate to ask me again in the future." Here's another one: "Actually, I am unable to make a commitment like that at this time. Thank you for thinking of me. I appreciate being included." Feel free to steal both responses and make them your own. They work, and in a very short period of time you'll feel the fruits of your effort.

The second year of my theme living was "Getting Things Done." I stumbled across a book with the same title by a fantastic writer, David Allen. I chose my theme before my first encounter with his book, so when I spied it at my local bookstore, it jumped off the shelf as if he had written it for me. His audio guide was so packed full of information on getting control of clutter that I couldn't listen to it while driving because I needed to take notes. I actually sat at my desk one day and listened to it for several hours, taking notes the whole way through. That was a first for me and I am still using the techniques I learned long after that year had passed.

The third year was "The Year of Tom," my husband of over twenty years. My idea was to make everything about *him*. He thought it was a great year; I thought it was a little long. The fourth year was the "The Year of Fun." We made a family list of things we wanted to do at some point during the year and then checked them off as we completed them. What a great year!

This leads me to my fifth year of my theme living: "The Year of Compassion." Simply put, when an opportunity arose to be kinder, or to help a stranger with a simple task, I stepped up. It was a revelation. I found a way to help someone almost daily; I just needed to be aware. My efforts were simple things like helping a short person reach a two-liter soda bottle on the top shelf at the grocery store, or helping someone lift a heavy bag into the overhead compartment of an airplane. Doing something without wanting anything in return is remarkable.

The year was going great until early October, when compassion turned to trouble for the person I was so eager to assist. Heading back from a trip to Buffalo, I arrived at my home airport in Chicago. The passenger tram that stops at each terminal and remote parking was packed. The tram has five stops each way and the system can be confusing to out-of-town travelers.

On this day, I was riding the tram out to the parking lot. I was engrossed in my paperback novel and not paying attention to my surroundings. Right before the doors closed, a woman jumped on board dragging two overstuffed designer suitcases. She was decked out in garments that looked more appropriate for Beverly Hills than Airportville. Her heels must have been at least six inches tall, a travel shoe I will never understand. She wore more jewelry than I own, even if I count my grade school mood ring. While she stumbled, dragged, and cursed her way on board, she was yelling into her cell phone, which was wedged between her cheek and shoulder in a no-hands hold. The rest of us couldn't help but overhear her conversation about how "rude the people of Chicago are!" She couldn't figure out the "forsaken place" and if she didn't hurry, she was going to miss her flight to Switzerland. There was some foul language involved too, which added to the show.

She wiggled into a spot next to me trying to keep her balance while the tram departed for the next station. I kept reading and tried to ignore her while she continued her heated monologue about her travel woes. As we pulled into the next station, I mistakenly thought we were at the International Terminal. I was so confident of my bearings, I didn't even look up. I just kept reading. "Gucci" made no move to get off the tram and I was concerned that she didn't realize that this was the stop for her international flight. A very brief internal debate unfolded as I tried to decide whether to keep quiet or speak. Because it was the year of compassion, I pushed myself to assist. Right before the doors closed, I interrupted her cell conversation and urgently blurted out, "Hey! This is your stop, Go! Go!" Seeing me frantically cranking my arm around like a traffic cop, she panicked. She slammed her phone shut, grabbed her bags and jumped out, barely clearing the doors. As we smoothly glided away, I saw her running full speed for the gates, or at least full speed for someone in stilettos. The volume inside the tram was hushed when a businessman next to me stated real slow and quiet, "Um, I think we were only at Terminal 2." (Which is two stops from where she needed to be.)

Glancing back, I saw the bright orange sign with a gigantic "2" float past the window. The look of shock and guilt on my face must have been hysterical because everyone started to laugh. Between fits of giggles, the woman on my left uttered, "Man, is she going to be pissed at you!" That incident led me to my theme for the following year: "The Year of Mind Your Own Stinkin' Business!"

After telling this story for several years, I've had some people report back to me on the themes they have chosen. There are some very creative people out there, but my favorite goes to a woman near Omaha who said, "My theme for the year is to achieve a 'Fat Checkbook and a Slim Ass'; unfortunately, last year I had it backwards." So what's your theme going to be for the next 365 days? Finding the perfect theme may be just what it takes to rejuvenate yourself and create a fun way to get focused.

P.S. Gucci Lady, if you are reading this
and recognize yourself in the story,
my deepest apologies for my bad advice.
Hope you made your flight somehow.

_____ a s k   y o u r s e l f . . .

What's the theme that I most want to live for this coming year?

What's a plan for bringing your theme to life?

What's the energy you already feel surrounding your creation?

"The true measure
of a man is how
he treats someone
who can do him
absolutely no good."

~Attributed to Samuel Johnson
English Writer and Lexicographer
1709–1784

What Does a "More Loving Life" Really Mean?

During my research for this book, I surveyed many people inquiring what they might ask themselves on a personal retreat. One friend wrote, "How can I be more loving?" Searching back through years of retreat notebooks, I was stunned to find out that I have never contemplated this question. I honestly didn't think there was a fundamental question that I hadn't noodled on at one time or another.

How can one be more loving? I reflect on my husband Tom and his ability to be loving. When I list his attributes, it defines loving for me. He is considerate, speaks nicely, shows interest, defends, laughs with, encourages, and shows compassion.

Being considerate is so important on the list of loving attributes. For example, Tom loves cold sheets at night. I'm the opposite. He knows what compromise is all about so one cold winter he gifted me with a dual-controlled electric blanket, even though he dislikes them. I was so grateful. That night, I set my side to level six and shuffled into the bathroom to prep for sleep. His thermostat control remained in the off position since he was already worried about the mass quantity of heat seepage expected from my side. I jumped in a few minutes later, anticipating a wave of warmth that tickles the spine like the feeling of gliding into a hot tub on a freezing winter night. I was surprised to find only a tepid condition. Tom was already trying to sleep, so instead of questioning the quality of the blanket, I just cranked it up to ten and slid down deeper into the sheets. A few minutes later, Tom threw back the covers, sweating and flushed, exclaiming, "I can't take it. I'm on fire over here!" We turned on the lights to investigate the cause of the one-sided burning bed. I realized I had placed the blanket on the mattress upside down, meaning my thermostat was controlling *his side* of the bed!

Sometimes being considerate of others requires personal sacrifice. Tom's consideration and compassion are two of his strongest and most attractive traits, and I hope our children develop the same character strengths as they mature.

When you are on the receiving end of compassion it's felt at a deep level that is memorable. For example, several years ago, Larry, a dear friend of ours, lost his mother to cancer. Her visitation was out of state and the family did not expect us to make the trip. However, we wanted Larry and his brothers to know we supported them in their time of grief. When we walked into the funeral home, Larry gave me a hug and said, "You didn't have to come all the way up here."

I quietly replied, "We would go anywhere we need to."

We showed up and Larry and his family felt our love and compassion. Three days later, our basement flooded due to a failed sump pump. We called Larry to borrow his extra pump. He insisted on bringing it over even though he had just gotten home from a long week with limited rest. I thought he would just drop it off, but the next thing I know, he's in the basement, helping to bail water and pull up wet carpet. I walked over and firmly said, "Hey, you *do not* need to stay and help with this. Go home and get your rest."

Without skipping a beat Larry quietly replied, "I'd go anywhere I need to."

These simple words boomeranged back at me, illustrating that there is great power in our actions; sometimes even very small gestures reverberate for years.

What I learned that day is that there is never a wrong time to show your support for others. There are always ways that we can be more helpful and more considerate.

I know I don't do enough to show others how much they are loved.
Do you?

_____ ask yourself...

In what specific way do I currently show love to others in my life?

Ask yourself *out loud*, "How can I show others my consideration and love in ways important to each of them?"

How do I want others to show their love to me? Do they know this?

"As I soak in the
quietness, as I bask in my
connection with life,
I realize these are
unbeatable moments."

~Leo Babuta
Author

Finding Focus:
Using the Five Senses

Silence. No distraction, expectation, noise, obligation, or anticipation. This is the ultimate mindset and environment for living in the here and now. I've always liked quiet, and it is the best way I've found to get "normal" back when my life feels off track.

When I was preparing my workstation to write this segment, I was already anticipating the calm of the moment. I'd gotten the family off to their proper locations for the day, so with a hot cup of tea in hand, a view of the world through my windows, and comfy clothes, I was ready to sparkle. Once in a while, I consciously become aware of all of my five senses and today seemed like a good day to acknowledge them. The following exercise is enacted by focusing on one sense at a time; sight, smell, touch, taste, and sound.

Begin by blocking out four senses, which elevates your awareness of the featured sense. Sometimes amazing things come to mind. At other times it is simply a meditative effort.

Allow your mind to drift from one thought to another. If you start to lose focus with a "to-do thought," then say out loud, PAUSE. Then take the time to write down the thought if necessary, in order to get it out of your mind. Begin again with a new focus point or shift to a new sense on which to concentrate.

Let me demonstrate how this works by transcribing my thoughts as they occurred during a five senses exercise.

SIGHT

There's a bright glare from the sun when I look out the windows. A late March snow hit yesterday and it remains on the ground. Disappointing, since I thought spring was here. I love spring and fall; dislike winter. I would like to move somewhere warm in the next fifteen years. We need to start researching possible locations soon. PAUSE. Add *research retirement* to action list. Now, regain focus.

My office is cluttered. It makes me feel out of control. There is a lot to be done. When I am done writing this chapter, I will tackle the piles and see what lurks for me in the mess. PAUSE. Add *clean office* to action list.

Focus on the candle flame. It flickers as I stare. When I am perfectly still, it calms. When I type quickly, it dances. The faster I move, the more violent the dance. Great metaphor. I should write that in the idea file for a future keynote on stress and maybe create an exercise out of flames. PAUSE. Add *work idea* to action list.

SMELL

My hands smell of the conditioner I just used on my hair. It smells clean, and I like clean. Ironic since I am sitting in a mess. PAUSE. It's already on the action list; stop focusing negative energy on this issue. Breathe in deep; breathe out. Today it isn't so much about what I smell; it is more about the peace and focus that comes with the deep breathing. Relaxing and comforting. (Try it yourself right now and really experience it.)

TASTE

I can still taste the healthy breakfast I ate and it makes me feel in control. Instead of bagels and cream cheese or a gigantic pastry, I am satisfied by my better choice. I'm drinking a cup of tea that is brewed by the cup. It has a robust flavor. Slightly sweet with a bitter chase. The best of both worlds.

SOUND

I can hear the constant whirl of the computer fan. There is an occasional car that goes by on our street. A dog barks outside. I should take our dog for a walk when I am done here. PAUSE. Add *walk our dog* to action list and refocus. When things are quiet and I focus on my breathing at the same time, I feel my stress decline. I need to make time to do this more often. It helps my thoughts get into the proper formation. Our lives are so busy we forget this very simple exercise.

TOUCH

A smooth rock from Door County, Wisconsin sits on my desk. It doesn't serve a purpose except to remind me of a wonderful afternoon spent skipping rocks across the water. Laughing, talking, sitting, and connecting with my future husband. The rock is pure white, not one scratch of color on it anywhere. It is so smooth you would think the waves of Green Bay had tossed it for a million years like nature's rock tumbler. When I glide the tips of my fingers lightly over its smooth surface, I am taken back to a simpler time. Less responsibility, more free time, less worry, more dreaming.

Sometimes life today feels more like a piece of coral
than a smooth stone.

I'd like to challenge you to become more aware by isolating each of your five senses. Stop for a few minutes and begin where you are now, or, take a walk. See what thoughts come to you. An "ah-ha moment" may be waiting for you. Remember to say PAUSE out loud when a thought takes you down a "should" trail or distracts you from the exercise at hand.

Another type of adventure to consider is a silent retreat. Years ago, I ran across an article about a location designed for silent retreat weekends.

There, one could explore thoughts, relax, meditate, or anything else one wanted to do, without making a sound. Some of the locations profiled in the article sounded delightful, but came with a hefty price tag. Others seemed reasonable, but were not quite the atmosphere I wanted.

However, one day a perfect juncture of dates appeared on my calendar. My teenage son was scheduled to attend a class trip to Washington D.C. and my husband and daughter had planned their annual daddy-daughter weekend getaway for the same time period. That meant that for the first time in almost eighteen years, I would be alone in the house for an extended period of time. That had opportunity for a silent retreat written all over it.

Soon, I had told many friends about my plan of twenty-four hours of silence. No sound in and no sound out could be a challenge for someone like me who loves to talk. In fact, I was talking about this nonstop for weeks before the event. A stranger at the florist overheard me sharing my idea with the owner and stepped over to tell me I had just given her a great idea she was going to use! How fun!

Several people I talked with shared what they would do with a full day of silence. Clean, sort, read, sleep, eat, fast, and exercise were some of their responses. I am the type of person who wants to use my time to think, plan, write, and relax. A year later I was still reaping the benefits of the decisions I made during my silent retreat. It sounds like I am exaggerating if I say it was a "life-changing day," but it's true. Early readers of my manuscript thought I should share the specifics of what was life changing, but I disagreed. Why? Because I feel that my results have no value or relevance to your needs. We will all experience something different on a silent retreat so I hesitate to put any ideas into your head. Please consider trying a silent retreat and then let me know what it did for you. I am so interested to hear.

In the absence of quiet, the mind cannot hear.

_____ ask yourself...

What observations did I make during the five-senses challenge?

Sight:

Smell:

Taste:

Sound:

Touch:

What "ah-ha moments" deserve more reflection?

"Tell a man there are
300 billion stars
in the universe and
he'll believe you.
Tell him a bench has
wet paint on it
and he'll have to touch
it to be sure."

~Anonymous

The Big Cookie

In yet another attempt to control my lack of discipline regarding food, I was given a specific suggestion by a friend who suggested I say STOP! out loud whenever the thought of eating unhealthy food came to mind. This helps the brain learn a new direction that in time may even become automatic.

So, the next day I am on the open highway on my way to a speaking engagement. I see a restaurant sign from a place known for its outstanding frozen custard. My mouth watered as I considered vanilla or strawberry, or maybe, the flavor of the day. Then I decided to try my friend's word association suggestion. Alone in the car, I said, "Laurie, stop! You do not need ice cream." Fortunately, it worked and I flew by that exit doing seventy-five miles per hour with a smile on my face.

One week later, I am headed to Des Moines, Iowa. This time my travel buddy, Lauren, is along. This is how I remember the events unfolding. I share my STOP! stories of the past seven days, of which there were plenty, and she agrees to try the system. We arrive at the hotel late and hungry. I dial room service and find out the kitchen is closed, but we can still get dessert. The gentleman on the phone proceeds to describe the house special, The Big Cookie Supreme. Get this: the special dessert was a pizza-sized chocolate chip cookie, topped with ice cream, hot fudge, whipped cream, and shaved chocolate. It comes warm and guaranteed in fifteen minutes or less. I repeat these details out loud to confirm with the man on the phone. Meanwhile, Lauren is shaking her head no and whispering, "Stop! Stop!" I wave her off. She steps closer and whispers a little louder, "Stop! No!" I turn my back on her and with the last ounce of self-discipline I possess, I say to the room service man, "Never mind, we are going to pass," and I sadly hang up the phone. Instead, we ate pretzels from the vending machine, which I found very unsatisfying, but at least I was proud of my self-control.

As we are leaving the next day, the meeting planner hands Lauren a container saying, "Here's a little treat for the road." We thank her and head on our way. About a mile out of town, I inquire about our gift. Lauren digs out the container, pops open the lid, and inside we find the signature dessert, The Big Cookie! I look to the heavens and say in exasperation, "Are you kidding me with this?" With five hours to drive and willpower gone, we shrug and dig into the temptation. It is one of the worst cookies I have ever tasted. At our next stop, we toss it in the gas station trash and laugh about how our impression and reality were so different.

How are your impression and your reality different? As I've traveled the country and met thousands of people through my work, the one constant I have found is that reality is obscure. A manager will believe his staff doesn't care about the organization. On the flip side, the staff is convinced the manager only cares about himself. They each are so cemented in their own reality that the truth is hidden and difficult to harvest. If I can get each side to release assumptions, give each other the benefit of the doubt, and appeal to their desire to find a solution, then we have a chance of successful mediation.

On a personal retreat, one would think it would be easier to reach a positive conclusion since it is a one-sided debate. But, in fact, it can be harder. Harder because softening your own convictions while alone in your thoughts is like boxing without a partner. You can practice your jabs and ducks all day long, but until you spar with a real opponent, it is tough to imagine what a punch to your jaw really feels like.

How are your assumptions and reality different?

Think of a situation where improvement is desired. This can be in a relationship, a work struggle or a personal battle. Take time to journal the answers to the questions below and see if you can shift the angle of your view and create a new outcome.

—————————————————————————— a s k   y o u r s e l f . . .

What assumptions have I made regarding this situation or challenge?

Are any of these assumptions fact?

In what ways can I give the benefit of the doubt to others involved in this situation?

If I need to appeal to their desire for solution, what words might I use to explain?

(Avoid using the word *you* and substitute the word *we*.)

"For every minute you
are angry you lose sixty
seconds of happiness."

~Ralph Waldo Emerson
American Poet and Essayist
1803–1882

Mosaic Masterpiece

My mother passed away in November of 2010 after fifteen years of poor health. She had the chance to read the first draft of this book and was helpful with edits and suggestions. I'm sad that the final manuscript never got the chance to meet her. When it was time to plan her memorial service, I stumbled across a challenge. When she was alive she was adamant about no picture boards at the funeral. She made me promise I wouldn't shroud the visitation with a wall of photos. Even if I had wanted to create a pictorial walk down memory lane, it would have been difficult. I can probably fill one small box with the photos we have of my mother because she never enjoyed having her picture taken. It was hard coming up with a way to give tribute to who she was and what was important to her without using photos. I finally decided to fill a basket with items that, when pieced together, would be a mosaic of who Joan Dannewitz was during her seventy-eight years on this planet.

I included a scorecard from her best-ever round of golf, her trophy for a hole-in-one, my grandfather's shaving cup that she once told me she cherished. I added a plate from her Depression Era glass collection handed down from my grandmother, a cribbage board that has great sentimental value to my folks, a crossword puzzle dictionary with her last half-done puzzles sticking out between the worn pages, a tiny photo of my father as a small boy that she always said was her favorite. The fabric in the bottom of the basket was black with red dice as a tribute to the hours of games she played with me as a child and with the grandchildren that followed. I wanted to hide a pack of Winston cigarettes under the fabric, but my brother thought it would be in bad taste. I think my mom would have enjoyed the humor and it certainly isn't a real mosaic of her without it. She was a fun lady and I miss her.

Reflecting back on Mom's Mosaic, I started to wonder what symbols create a mosaic of me? After much thought and editing, a list of ten symbols that would represent me remained:

- Family photos
- Ocean
- Games
- Bright colors, as many as possible
- Interesting conversation with people I care about
- Slippers
- Hot tea
- Sunglasses
- Golf clubs
- Diet Coke, extra ice, slice of lemon

I tried to resist writing down the last entry on my list because it seems silly. But alas, this is a book of truth and anyone who knows me knows it wouldn't be a completed mosaic of me without it!

A friend recently shared her observation with me after doing this exercise. She thought about what symbols she would like to have in her mosaic, and a horse was one of them. However, she has not been around horses in years. It dawned on her that maybe she should be making time for a new hobby. She doesn't have to own a horse to enjoy the experience of riding. I think many of us have items that probably belong in our basket that we haven't made room for in our daily lives.

Each great moment of life links together
to form your mosaic masterpiece.

Now, it's your turn. Create your list of ten things that, when pieced together, make your life's mosaic. When you are done, come back to answer the questions below.

_____ ask yourself...

Was it hard to make the list of symbols that represent me?

If so, why?

Were there items I wanted to put on the list, but resisted?

If so, why?

What else do I want to include in my life's mosaic?

Exercise
———————— no.10 ————————

Lifeline List

One of best ways to rejuvenate yourself, especially if you feel alone, is to create a lifeline list. Learning how to ask for what we want is a skill that takes practice. While sharing this concept at a speaking engagement years ago, a conference attendee shared her feeling on this:

> Nobody offers what you don't request. Want a better view at the hotel you just checked into? Ask. Need a spouse to help out more? Ask, and be specific. Wishing this committee would step up their efforts? It's time for me to ask!

Her bold participation led more people to agree to help on their next outreach effort as a committee. Ask for what you want.

Make a list of ten people who believe in you and would be more than willing to help you on your personal journey. If you have trouble thinking of ten people, scroll through your cell phone contacts. It may trigger a perfect match.

Now, write a specific request for help that you might make of each person on the list. This is not to say you will ask for it. It's just an exercise in thinking about what you need from other people and forming the words to ask. If you do decide to act on any of the requests, it may help you to start your sentence with, "I need your assistance and I am hoping you will agree to help me (insert action)."

Exercise

no.11

Symbolic Crafting

This crafty exercise is a must for readers who enjoy gathering symbolic items and creating a homemade masterpiece. I especially enjoy this activity if I need a break from mental calisthenics and, instead, want to relax in good thoughts. Gather items that symbolize feelings, people, events, goals, memories, or anything else that helps you rejuvenate and celebrate your life. Here are several examples of symbolic crafting that either my fellow retreaters or I have done.

- Shop at an antique or flea market and gather small inexpensive items that represent your concept and place them in a shadow box.

- Scrapbook with photos or pictures.

- Visit a bead store and select unusual shapes, colors, or styles of beads or charms, and make a bracelet or necklace.

- Fill a vase with items. A friend who was ill received one of these from a group of her friends. It was filled with items that represented healing as well as specific tokens of their relationship with her.

- Go on an outdoor scavenger hunt. Pick up items from nature and turn them into a sculpture.

- Embark on a photo adventure. Take pictures that are symbolic of your life.

- Paint on canvas even if you aren't an artist.

Exercise

—————————— no.12 ——————————

Author for the Day

My final exercise is to ask you to be a writer. Even if you have never considered being an author, try being one today. Write one chapter about a time you learned a lesson about yourself. What questions could a reader ask themselves that tie in with your story?

Don't worry about being a great writer; just write. When you are done, please consider sending your thoughts to me or sharing them on our website found at www.WrappedInStillness.com.

It's hard to know when a book like this is "done" because the stories and neat things people share never end. I can't wait to hear from you. Who knows, maybe your thoughts will end up in my next book for others to enjoy or, better yet, be inspired to write one of your own.

_____ thoughts...

Wrap Up & Resources

Closing Ceremony

The closing ceremony of your personal retreat is important. Many people like to plan a closing ceremony that matches their opening ceremony. Others prefer concluding in prayer, thanksgiving, or meditation. Just like your opening ceremony, it doesn't matter what you do as long as it brings appropriate closure to the time you've invested in yourself.

Try to walk away from your personal retreat with follow-up actions or personal intentions for the coming months. Create a list of the questions for yourself and gradually dig deeper or narrow down the scope of your answers until you arrive at your core GO-Qs. These are the questions you take home to ponder and hopefully answer. These are the action steps you hopefully take. The list of intentions and concerns you assembled is your inner voice telling you what you've known but needed to acknowledge.

Here is an example of a list of concerns provided by a recent personal retreat attendee:

- Why am I unhappy?

- Am I the cause of this unhappiness?

- Why can't I get past this down feeling?

- What will it take to get back the person I used to be?

Certainly the closing ceremony is not mandatory, but it's a nice way to build a bridge back to your daily activities and complete your personal retreat experience.

I choose to keep my closing ceremony very simple. I write a plan for the post-retreat, stating my core intention out loud, and extinguish the flame of my centering candle. That's it. Simple.

A friend, who dances as hard and fast as she can to her favorite tune, finds dancing alone to be the ultimate in freedom of expression, so she closes her personal retreat in this way.

Another friend fills a deep tub with hot water and adds bubble bath and her long list of stressors. When the water chills and she's finished soaking, she pulls the plug and watches the water drain slowly while visualizing her stressors flowing down with it. She told me of the joy and lightheartedness she feels when the last drop gurgles away.

Regardless of your routine, the most critical element of closing your retreat is your mindset on departure. What separates a personal retreat from a vacation day is internal reflection and the action steps you take when you return to daily life. One small change for the better will create a ripple effect, the power of which you may not even realize at first.

After Your Personal Retreat

Hopefully, your personal retreat provided a break from life's fast ride.

Rosie O'Donnell once said, "A person is only as good as her brakes, just like any other forward moving machine." The day I read her quote, a light bulb went on in my head. It reminded me that I actually have the ability to put on the brakes *by taking a break!* At the time, I was filled with obligations and distractions, obliviousness and discomforts. My days were full, yet little was being accomplished. For a long time, I talked about making a change, but all talk and no follow-through had become my bumper sticker. It was April when I read Rosie's quote, so I decided to officially slam on the breaks. I deemed May of 2011 the "month of no distractions." What that meant is that for thirty days I wouldn't make unnecessary phone calls, go to lunch with friends, agree to any obligation that wasn't already on the calendar and most importantly, my time would be spent on focused activity. Included on my list of tasks were some "guilt-free" shutdown blocks of time. Want to take a nap on a Sunday afternoon, do it! Want to read in the hammock as the sun is going down, do it! When analyzing Rosie's metaphor a little further, it became clear to me that when we slow down the ride, the scenery is easier to enjoy. Cliché? Sure it is, but it doesn't make it any less true.

One of my all-time favorite bosses, Annette McMichael, shared a story about slowing down with me.

My husband and I are partners in business as well as life. Since we have been so focused on business and family over the years, we haven't taken a vacation alone together for a long time. Our last getaways were spent visiting our grown children or vacationing with them. We finally managed to enjoy a seven-day hiking trip on the Colorado Plateau. As soon as we arrived, we agreed to put on the business and family brakes. A strange thing happened. We started liking each other just as we had when we first met. I mean, genuinely liking each other for the people we are, not for the roles we play as business partners, housemates, and parents. A funny thing happened on our last day of vacation. We'd left the North Rim of the Grand Canyon, and I was driving to our final stop. We were flying home the next morning, and my mind was already on the stack of work that was, no doubt, waiting for me. I was attempting to stay within the speed limit of Highway 89, but as I came over a hill and saw the state trooper I realized I was doing sixty-seven in a fifty-five. Sorry to say, despite the fact that I'm a little gray-haired woman and tried to plead my case, I couldn't get out of the ticket. I realized later that it was an excellent reminder to keep my life moving in the slow lane.

When I think of slowing down, I think of creating quiet. I mean quiet within the room and most importantly, quiet within my head. Silence can become a presence in the room if you allow it. It is rare that I use Webster's definitions when speaking or writing, but as I write this chapter, I cannot resist, because the defined meaning of the word *braking* is so perfect for the message I am trying to convey.

Take a look at a few of the definitions:

- A device for slowing or stopping by the absorption or transfer of energy

- Anything that has a slowing or stopping effect

And now look at a few of the 122 definitions for the word *breaking*:

- To put an end to; overcome; stop

- Overcome or wear down the spirit

- To interrupt the regularity

Now that your personal retreat is over, it is important to reflect back on the time away from your daily life and time demands. Did your retreat help you realize you need a break from something? How can you apply the brake to your life? Are there areas that need to be stopped for good, rather than just being placed on pause? If yes, what are the consequences of stopping?

Abraham Lincoln once said that, "People are just about as happy as they make their minds up to be." That seems honest to me. Now is the time to be honest with yourself and put on the brakes where and when you need to. After your personal retreat, it is important you take the action steps focused on fulfilling your needs. Otherwise, the pace of a daily life quickly seeps back in and may prevent you from obtaining the true value of your personal retreat. Refer back to the chapters and the passages you highlighted when they popped out at you. Try to use this book as a breathing instrument that moves with you and helps you keep your focus long after your personal retreat is over.

Final Thoughts

After a while, constant pondering, self-examination, and internal criticism must be put aside. Stagnation sets in if you sit idle for too long. So take your action list and *act!* One little action step focused on fulfilling the goal of each of your entries will allow you to start living your thoughts instead of just thinking and wishing.

This is the day of reckoning.
It is the time when I am called to account for my actions,
and fulfill my promises to myself.

As you are nearing the end of this journey, there are important questions to ask yourself so that the time spent transfers to "life out there." What good feelings do you have right now that will be difficult to maintain when your personal retreat is over? Why?

Are your thoughts meant to inspire action, or are they meant to be protected in your mind, heart, and soul?

If action is your answer, determine the specific steps needed and attach a deadline to each. If you have decided that only contemplation is best, ask yourself *why is this best*? Certainly the exercises of answering tough questions at the end of each chapter led you to a few eye-opening moments. Please take time to do the important task that follows.

I would like you to set a timer for fifteen minutes and then write (or type) your thoughts about your personal retreat non-stop until the timer beeps.

Don't concern yourself with penmanship, typos, spelling, grammar, clarity, or worry what others might think. Allow yourself to be in the moment and go where your thoughts take you. When you are done, read it, fold it, and put it away somewhere safe to refer to another time. As you may have a noticed, a majority of this book is made up of action steps I hope you will take. In this exercise, I ask for no additional action. Just write. You may find the reflection of the new you just waiting to emerge off the page.

I wish I were there to enjoy this with you. Hopefully, my book has been the friend you need.

Know without a doubt, you are worthy of acceptance.

thoughts...

Sample Agenda for a One-Day Personal Retreat

CREATE THE SPACE

Assemble your items in the general area where you plan to center yourself. Take care of all necessary loose ends before beginning. Make any last minute phone calls. Then, unplug or turn off the device and remove distractions like computer access.

START THE RETREAT WITH AN ACTION

A specific movement can help you bridge from your current state of mind into personal retreat mode, for example, taking a walk, reading a special poem or scripture, writing in a journal, meditating, or creating an opening ceremony.

OPENING CEREMONY

This optional two-to-fifteen minute activity helps you center your attention and bridge your focus from a regular day into a personal retreat day. Not all people use a focus moment to prepare, but I encourage you to try. Easy options include lighting a candle, praying, singing/humming, talking out loud, dancing, stretching, or deep breathing.

SAY YOUR INTENTION OUT LOUD

Is there a specific question you want to focus on during this retreat? Speak your question out loud or write it down and post it where you can glance at it the whole time as a centering point.

READ THE CHAPTERS THAT APPEAL TO YOUR CURRENT NEEDS

Refer to the table of contents to find the chapters that best match the intention of your personal retreat. Please note that reading chapters without taking the time to process and answer the questions will not provide the best insight for your day.

WHEN YOU FIRST FEEL RESTLESS, DISTRACTED, OR TIRED, GET UP AND MOVE

Listen to what your body is telling you it needs. Change your environment. If you are retreating inside, then step out for some fresh air. If you are retreating outside, go inside for a moment. Enjoy a favorite food, beverage, or relax by meditating or taking a short nap.

CHOOSE ONE RETREAT EXERCISE AT THE HALFWAY POINT OF YOUR DAY

This changes your thinking and your viewpoint. Often people return to the second half of their personal retreat more inspired. Don't limit yourself to the ideas in the book. I know many people who enjoy a craft project or create a vision board as ways to shift gears during a retreat.

IN THE LATER PHASE OF YOUR RETREAT, TAKE TIME TO REVIEW

Read back through your journal, reflect, and create a page of final thoughts or a plan of action following your personal retreat, if applicable.

CLOSING CEREMONY

Taking two to fifteen minutes to state your action plan out loud helps solidify your exit intention. Extinguish flames, pack your supplies, and close out your retreat with positive and self-congratulatory thoughts. You've had a good day and you deserved it.

AUTHOR LAURIE GUEST is a gifted facilitator, helping thousands of people through her speeches and retreats for individuals, entrepreneurs, and corporations. Clients say she has the rare ability to ask just the right questions to create breakthrough insights. She's learned how to do this because she grapples with similar challenges to her retreat participants: how to live an aware and honest life amid the intrusions and demands life tosses at us.

Laurie honed her communication style during her twenty-four years in health care and two decades as a business owner. For twenty years, she's been a highly rated facilitator and speaker. She specializes in sharing the lessons she's learned to help others in their professional and personal lives, overcoming obstacles and increasing positive outlooks and productivity.

She wrote this book to provide guidance to anyone wanting to lead a more fulfilling life. She's used the activities in it for her own personal growth as well as in her in-person retreats.

For more info on how Laurie could lead a retreat or speak to your group, contact her at:

Laurie@SolutionsAreBrewing.com

Made in the USA
San Bernardino, CA
07 July 2016